BLOOD KNOTS

'A stunning memoir of a childhood spent in search of fish in England… I'll quote Danny Finkelstein, a judge on the Samuel Johnson Prize, who tweeted after it made the shortlist: "Luke Jennings did the impossible with *Blood Knots* – he made me excited and moved by fishing."' Ruaridh Nicoll, *Observer* Summer Reading

'*Blood Knots* is an exceptional book. More than simply a memoir of angling, it is in fact a book about history and war, about affection and loss, memory and place. Written in precise, beautiful language, it is as thoughtful and profound in its descriptions of people and events as of fishing in settings both rural and urban. Deeply and essentially English in its evocations and sensibility, it is in the finest traditions of both nature and memoir writing – in short, it is a classic – a book that will be read for a long time, and treasured.' Esther Woolfson, author of *Corvus: A Life with Birds*

'I was transfixed. Hooked, even. *Blood Knots* is a beautifully crafted story, a masterclass in gilded loss. I was completely absorbed by Jennings' stilled, naturalist's eye as he waited by dark canals and chuckling chalk streams for that flash of beauty, while on that other plane, above the water, the ugly chaos of life waited to resume its infernal narrative. Haunting.' Nicholas Crane

'Luke Jennings has produced an eloquent and deeply moving angling memoir… This is a tale about a lost world occupied by ghosts… It is a book about the mysteries of Catholicism and of the dark arts of country pursuits, of mass, monks and inspirational masters, of hooded falcons, big skies, atmospheric waters and of a lonely planet… I can happily say that this is my book of the year… If you are an angler you will love it and if you are not you will devour it and may understand why others are.' John Andrews, www. caughtbytheriver.net

'Takes the reader into the world of the complete angler. The author shares the peace and tranquility of the banks of the canal, river, pond and lake with the rustle and swaying of reeds and deep brooding waters, full of dark mystery… A beautifully written work.' Geoffrey Wellum, author of *First Light*

'Nothing prepared me to be so gripped by Luke Jennings' memoir of his boyhood struggles to catch freshwater fish. He interweaves edge-of-the-seat tales of angling with profound meditations, wry anecdotes and, at the book's heart, moving valedictories to the two extraordinary men who were his role models.' Catherine Mayer, *Time* London Bureau Chief

'Written by a true fisherman, seeking something more than the most challenging fish – a spiritual dimension. *Blood Knots* can suddenly turn a corner and take you by surprise. Time will lodge this somehow reticent *tour de force* firmly in fishing literature's pantheon.' *Country Life*

Blood Knots

A Memoir of Fishing and Friendship

LUKE JENNINGS

Atlantic Books
LONDON

First published in hardback and export and airside trade
paperback in Great Britain in 2010 by Atlantic Books,
an imprint of Atlantic Books Ltd.

This paperback edition published by Atlantic Books in 2011.

The author and publisher would gratefully like to acknowledge the following
for permission to quote from copyrighted material: 'Burnt Norton' from 'Four
Quartets' in *Collected Poems 1909–1962* by T. S. Eliot, T. S. Eliot © 1944,
reproduced by permission of Faber & Faber for the author; 'The Pike' in
Collected Poems of Ted Hughes by Ted Hughes, Ted Hughes © 1960, reproduced
by permission of Faber & Faber for the author; *A River Runs Through It* by
Norman McLean, © 1976 by The University of Chicago, reproduced by
permission of The University of Chicago Press.

Every effort has been made to trace or contact all copyright holders. The
publishers will be pleased to make good any omissions or rectify any mistakes
brought to their attention at the earliest opportunity.

1 2 3 4 5 6 7 8 9 10

A CIP catalogue record for this book is available
from the British Library.

ISBN: 978 1 84887 133 5

Printed in Great Britain by CPI Bookmarque, Croydon

Illustrations by Caroline Church, © Caroline Church 2010

Atlantic Books
An Imprint of Atlantic Books Ltd
Ormond House
26–27 Boswell Street
London
WC1N 3JZ

www.atlantic-books.co.uk

To Nicky, Basil, Rafe and Laura, as always

BLOOD KNOTS

ONE

By closing time there's not much traffic going past the King's Cross goods yards; perhaps it's too late at night, or too close to Christmas. You can hear the distant rumble of the cars on the Euston Road, but in the yards it's quiet. And very cold.

To get to the canal you have to duck underneath an advertising hoarding and push open an iron gate; although this used to be padlocked, someone's taken a pair of bolt-cutters to it and now it just needs a good shove. Beyond it there's a railway maintenance supply area piled with concrete railway sleepers, rusted steel reinforcing rods and rectangles of welded wire mesh. Overlooking this are two low sheds. A pyramid of ceramic powerline insulators stands outside one of these and beside it a couple of figures are bowed over a flickering lighter. The tiny flame dies as I pass and then rekindles. There may be other people that I can't see. Some of the yard is lit by the sodium glare of the lights on Goods Way, whilst most of it is black shadow.

At the top of the yard there's the sharp smell of fox shit. The second gate's hard to see, concealed behind ragged bushes of sycamore and wild lilac, but I know it's there, just as I know to avoid the razor wire that loops above it. The gate swings open. In front of me, flat and metallic, is the canal, reflecting the Mars-red glow of the city. I stare at it for a moment, my breath vaporizing, and wonder whether to fish right here. It's deep at this point, a great tank of water held between banks of Victorian brick. Opposite me, on the far bank, is the dark mass of a disused warehouse, rusted bars guarding its long-broken windows. At its base, as if awaiting collection from the towpath, stands an old spin-dryer. Everything about the place suggests neglect. And big pike thrive on neglect.

However, it's not where I've come to fish. I've come to fish downstream of here, in a place I've been tipped off about. My source is Dejohn. Most fishermen will tell you anything, just for the hell and the geniality of it, but Dejohn's information is usually good. Aged fourteen and a habitual truant, he knows every inch of this stretch. We're not friends, exactly, but we talk.

I saw him a week ago at the Vale of Health Pond on Hampstead Heath. It was a Saturday afternoon, and the light was going. Dejohn had caught a small rudd and was using it as live-bait, illegally but excitingly drifting it across the pond beneath a fluorescent yellow float in the hope of enticing a pike. We swapped stories as usual and I told him that I'd heard that someone had landed half a dozen jack-pike weighing up to six pounds from a barge on the Kingsland Basin in de Beauvoir Town. Dejohn mused on this for a moment and then said that he'd heard – second-hand, but he trusted the source – about some bloke who'd been drinking in the Pentonville Road and at closing time, well pissed up, had decided to go fishing. So he'd hauled his gear out of the van, dragged it to the canal, set himself up with a dead-bait rig, and gone to sleep in his chair. At 3 a.m. he'd woken up to find line running off his reel, and had struck into a big fish. When he felt the weight of it, Dejohn said – and the dead, dour resistance of a really big pike is nothing like the angry jagging of a middle-weight fish – the hairs had gone up on the back of his neck. After a minute or so, during which the pike moved unstoppably upstream, the wire trace gave way and the guy was left there on the towpath, shaking like a leaf.

Now of course this story has all the elements of the classic pike myth. It's hearsay, it's uncheckable, and it involves a monster. But to me it has the ring of possibility, being chaotic and unheroic, as these things often are. And Dejohn has been specific as to the location. Specific to the nearest yard. I move carefully down-stream, watching my step in the near-darkness, past dim clumps of dead nettles and through a piss-smelling underpass. Distantly, there's the whisper of a sluice and the sound of swearing. It's a girl's voice, probably one of the teenage prostitutes who bring their punters down to the towpath – a cheaper if colder place to turn a trick than the local hotels.

I'm out of the underpass now. Above me, against the dull red of the sky, stand the skeletal outlines of the St Pancras gasworks. Soon, my rod and tackle bags bumping against me as I walk, I come to a low bridge and push through trailing brambles into the tunnel. I can see nothing in the darkness except the faint red semi-circle of the exit, but there's an echoing drip and the stone slabs are greasy beneath my feet. When a truck passes overhead with a booming shudder the drips fall faster.

At the far end, as I step out into the ambient light, the towpath and the canal widen. At my back, behind galvanized-steel security fencing and a ragged thicket of wild buddleia, is some kind of electrical installation. A steel sign on the fencing warns of power-grid cables beneath the towpath. In front of me is a long oblong of water, perhaps twenty feet across. Its surface rocks like molten copper. There is no far bank, just a high wall of mossy brick, weeping with damp. As I lower my gear to the paving stones, the cold immediately begins to fold around me. This is the place.

I set up quickly, keen to get my hands back into my gloves. I'm using an old fibreglass spinning-rod by Rudge of Redditch, heavy by today's standards but pretty much unbreakable. The reel, battered but well balanced, is an Aerial-style centre-pin. The baits are frozen sprats, mounted by a single treble-hook to wire traces. Pen-torch in mouth, I knot a trace to the fifteen-pound breaking-strain monofilament. A small coffin-lead goes between line and trace, to hold the bait to the bottom. It's the most straightforward rig possible. You don't want to get elaborate in the dark.

A final check. The red bulb of the pen-torch is bright enough to inspect the knots and swivels, but doesn't knock out my night vision. The landing net stands within reach against the bridge. The rod-rest is jammed securely into a crack between the glazed bricks at the towpath's edge. Stripping half a dozen yards of line from the reel, I send the sprat looping into the darkness. There is the faintest of splashes and I sense the coffin-lead sinking deeper and deeper, before, with a tiny slackening, it touches bottom. I reel in until the line is tight, engage the ratchet, lay the rod in the rest and sit down on my folding stool. Incline my back against the cold brickwork of the bridge. Wait.

To begin with, as always, I imagine how it will be. The twitch of the line at my index finger, the slow tick of the centre-pin's ratchet, the shudder of the rod as the fish runs. If it's big, I'll have a problem. The bottom of the canal is a catacomb of old bikes, shopping trolleys and other detritus. The pike will know every twist and turn, and if given an inch of line will bore down into the maze and smash up my tackle. I'll never even see it. And at the very least I'll want to see it, because there's something elemental in the first sight of a pike.

One overcast autumn morning I hooked one on the pond called Red Arches, on Hampstead Heath. A boy walking a dog saw the rod bucking in my hands and wandered up to watch. The fish kicked deep, going for the weed roots, but finally I brought it up. The water was coloured from the rain, so at first all that was visible was a dark shadow, but gradually you could make out the long back, the rapacious jaw, the slow fanning of the pectoral fins. When I had landed and unhooked it I held it up for a moment. River pike are olive-green, the colour of stones flecked with sunlight, but this was a deep-water fish, as dark and grim as old armour. Eyeing its teeth, meeting its unflinching gaze, the boy backed away.

'Jesus,' he breathed. 'What is that?'

I told him. And as I slid it back into the water I added that it wasn't particularly big, as they went. That there were pike there three times its size.

'Jesus,' he repeated, looking around him as if seeing the city for the first time.

As to the shape and proportion of this great devourer, the figure of his body is very long, his back broad, and almost square, equal to the lowest fins: his head is lean and very bony, which bones in his head, some have resembled to things of mysterious consequence; one of which they commonly compare to the cross, another to the spear, three others to the bloody nails which were the instruments of our Saviour's passions. (Robert Nobbes, *The Complete Troller*, 1682)

The cold hardens, and the first currents of wind come nosing down the canal from the east, burring the water's surface like an iron file. A few yards away, on the bridge, an occasional car passes, as if in another dimension. My world has contracted to a box of darkness: to the walls, the towpath and the black of the water. As always, there's the temptation to wind in the bait a little, to check that it's OK, but that way madness lies, because you'll never really know what's happening down there.

Nor would you want to, because in an over-illuminated world, a world whose dark corners are in constant retreat from the remorseless, banal march of progress, this not knowing is a thing to be valued and enjoyed. It may be that your hooks are caught in the rusting spokes of a bicycle wheel, that your bait has already been stripped from the hook by Chinese mitten-crabs, but this is the nature of fishing. The odds are almost overwhelmingly against you and that is how you like it. All that you can do is offer your bait to the water, empty your mind, and reach for your thermos, your hip flask and whatever other comforting poisons you've brought with you.

In other words, you must acknowledge the ritual nature of what you're doing. If a butterfly beats its wings in the Caribbean, they say, this can set in train a series of events culminating in a hurricane in the Pacific. Students of a post-modern form of occultism known as Chaos Magic take the idea further, suggesting that, under the proper conditions, this Butterfly Effect can be harnessed for wish-fulfilment. The technique involves a ritual consignment of the wish to the elements and an intense visualization of the required outcome. The dynamics of chaos will do the rest.

In the past, these ritual actions were often accompanied by invocations. One thought to be particularly effective was devised by the Elizabethan mage John Dee. It's written in the Enochian language, which, Dee claimed, was revealed to him by angels, with whom he and his fellow magician Edward Kelley regularly conversed. Usefully, Dee kept records of these exchanges, and a century later, in 1659, Meric Casaubon collected and published them under the title *A True and Faithful Relation of What Passed for Many Years between Dr John Dee and Some Spirits*. The book is in the British Library, a few hundred yards from where I'm fishing, and was the basis for the system of high ritual magic developed by the twentieth-century occultist Aleister Crowley for the Order of the Golden Dawn, the secret hermetic society of which he was a member. John Dee's invocation for wish-fulfilment ended with the following words:

SA CHAOS ANGELARD HARG AZIAGIAR.
OD IONAS.
(Into chaos the wish is cast. May it be harvested.)

You could try this when fishing: it certainly echoes every angler's intention. Some occultists favour adding to the invocation the mantra, *Zarzas Zarzas Nastana Zarzas*. These words, which are beyond translation, are said to summon Choronzon, the baleful Watcher of the Abyss. Crowley, who claimed to have raised Choronzon in the Algerian desert in 1909 (and to have terrified himself and his companion half witless in the process), advises against this. The wise angler will heed his counsel. Specimen coarse fish are one thing, the Dark Lord of Entropy quite another.

As it happens, there's a tenuous connection between Crowley and my family. In 1903, having met her just twenty-four hours earlier at a Scottish spa, Crowley absconded with Rose Kelly, the sister of the painter Gerald Kelly, and married her the same day. Furious, Kelly determined that the marriage be annulled. He knew Crowley well; the two men had met at Cambridge a few years earlier and were both marauding sexual adventurers. They had probably shared lovers in Paris the year before and may even have been lovers themselves (in letters to Kelly, Crowley sometimes signed himself Maud, although this in itself doesn't prove anything. Rod Stewart and Elton John used to call each other Sharon and Phyllis).

It didn't take a genius to guess that the Crowleys' marriage wasn't going to survive. The couple were divorced six years later in the wake of Crowley's persistent infidelity and cruelty, and Rose would eventually die an alcoholic. During these upsetting times Kelly was befriended and counselled by Harnett Ellison

Jennings, my great-grandfather, then the vicar of Dulwich. Perhaps it was out of gratitude that Kelly painted a fine, sombre, life-sized portrait of the Reverend Harnett robed as a Doctor of Divinity. We have it still.

In fact, Rose and Crowley were not completely incompatible. On their honeymoon they went to Ceylon, as it was then named, where Crowley took up shooting. Having discovered that the island's giant fruit bats were renowned for their soft belly fur, he decided to try and kill enough of them to make himself a waistcoat and Rose a hat. With his first shot, taken from a lakeside punt, a wounded bat fell on Rose. The experience had a profound effect on her and that night Crowley was awakened by a high-pitched squeaking. Lighting a candle, he found his wife hanging naked from the frame of the mosquito net. No one could accuse her of failing to get into the spirit of things.

We're drifting here, as you often do when fishing. Half of you is tensely expectant, while half of you enters a zone of no time at all. The question is: what does the angler wish for when he casts? What, as the chaos people might put it, is the willed endpoint of the working? On the surface, the answer appears simple: to catch a fish. You want to deceive a wild creature, take it from its element, marvel over it and return it to the wild. But that's only part of it – what you might call the ego element. The living, wriggling proof of your skill and cunning. Proof that, in the right circumstances, you can get one over the natural world.

For a time, that's what I thought it was all about. Success or failure. Statistics. The numbers game. The late Bernard Venables, author of the classic Mr Crabtree fishing books, used to say that there are three stages to the angler's evolution. To begin with, as a child, you just want to catch fish – any fish. Then you move to the stage where you want to catch big fish. And finally, with nothing left to prove, you reach a place where it's the manner of the catch that counts, the rigour and challenge of it, at which point the whole thing takes on an intellectual and perhaps even a philosophical cast. I tried out this theory on a pike-angling friend of mine, the rock guitarist René Berg. 'It's like with women, then?' he said thoughtfully.

We agreed that there was truth in the three-stage theory, but not the whole truth. The ego thing is certainly important. When I was a boy, and you stayed in a pub or hotel that had trout fishing attached to it, it was conventional to display the day's catch on a salver in the hall. It would have taken the Dalai Lama to ignore the competitive undercurrent. No one went so far as to add his name, but by dinnertime everyone knew who had caught what, and if you had laid out a decent fish you could expect a quiet 'Well done, old boy!' from the major as you sat down to the Brown Windsor soup.

Of course, most fishermen soon progress beyond the need to prove themselves and the desire to compile lists of statistics. Most soon realize that there are 'easy' fish, like small roach and perch, and subtle, challenging fish like carp or barbel. However, there is something fundamental beyond which the lifelong angler never quite progresses. Something for which the three-stage theory makes no allowances (although Venables himself, as his writing indirectly makes clear, was well aware of it). And that's what happens when you hook a big fish. A pike, especially.

The best big pike waters have a numinous, forbidding air. Cold, reed-fringed East Anglian meres. Desolate Irish loughs. Dark, secretive waters 'as deep as England', as Ted Hughes puts it. You feel that you're trespassing, that you're violating some natural law just by being there. Certain stretches of London waterways like the Regent's Canal and the River Lea fall into this category. These silent conduits barely figure in most local people's lives. As the years have passed they've become invisible, walled off from residential areas and the footpaths of commerce as if they present a danger. And perhaps they do: what could be more fatal to the garishly hyped-up business of consumption than, like a memento mori, a sudden glimpse of black water, sliding past as silent as the Styx? I will be here when your lifestyle accessories are landfill, such a vision promises. I will be here when the music ends.

For the fisherman, it's otherwise. For the fisherman, slipping behind the hoardings and picking his way over the vehicle scrap to the water's edge, it's like stepping into another world, at once familiar and resonantly strange. The notion of death is not absent there – anywhere you can cast a line, you can hear the whisper of Poussin's *Et in Arcadia Ego* – but then there's more than a touch of the gothic in most urban anglers, an appreciation that certain things are best illuminated by darkness.

Hidden from the public gaze, transfigured by changing circumstance, London's waterways have been absorbed into an alternate, morbid geography. An interzone where past and present have become compacted, and the wild and the man-made have assumed a new relationship. That some people are drawn to these places and that others are deeply wary of them is understandable. Since 1953, the year of my birth, there have been more than a dozen officially recorded murders on London towpaths. At night, with their dank concrete and rusting ironwork, they're the domain of fly-tippers, graffiti taggers, drug dealers, pimps and drunks. If you're fishing there, you have to watch yourself.

Even so, it's worth it. Take nocturnal possession of fifty feet of canal, tackle up for pike and sooner or later – not on your first visit, perhaps, or your second, but eventually – it will happen. The line will start to trickle, inch by cautious inch, from your reel. If you've got it set to ratchet, you will hear a click, and then another and another, and as you feel the line creep over the back of your hand, a kind of dread will rise through your body. Somewhere out there, deep down, something is moving.

You sweep up the rod and strike, there's a hard, angry swirl, and you're connected. Not to a fish, at that moment, but to something much less resolved. To nature itself. Nature as the source of the crocodile grin, the bloody cycle, the pitiless will to power. The experience, in those first brief moments, is demonic. The heart pounds and you feel an icy vacuum expanding inside you. And then, with a fierce thrill, you see the fish in the torchlight – the long flank and jaw, the cold flash of the eye, the furious working of the fins – and what follows is the physical, practical business of landing it. There's satisfaction in these later stages, of course, but it's those first heart-in-mouth seconds that you keep going back for. For the moment when anything is possible. When it might not be a fish at all.

The cold hardens. And staring into the dark water, its surface now the faint sodium orange of the sky, I imagine lean, predatory shadows moving between the brickwork walls as if patrolling a silent enfilade of rooms. Beneath them, a carpet of silt softens the forms of discarded household appliances, ranged like the prizes on some half-remembered TV quiz show. The image connects with a dream I've had, at intervals, ever since I was a child, in which I'm walking the streets of a deserted, once-grand city. As so often in dreams, it's night and day at the same time, and climbing the steps to one of the mansions at the roadside I find myself proceeding through a succession of halls dominated by enigmatic monuments. In steel, or perhaps black marble, these have a futuristic, fascistic appearance. Eventually, and with an overpowering sense of desolation, I arrive at a flight of stone steps lapped by waves. Before me is a vast inland sea, its waters extending to the limits of my vision.

It was with a strong sense of recognition that I first read James Thomson's poem 'The City of Dreadful Night', in which the narrator walks the streets of a necropolis – a 'Venice of the Black Sea' – past 'ranged mansions dark and still as tombs'.

> The city is not ruinous, although
> Great ruins of an unremembered past,
> With others of a few short years ago
> More sad, are found within its precincts vast...

There are places, invariably near bodies of water, where that sense of an unremembered past is particularly strong. Where you turn a corner and know for certain that you've been there before. Fishing, at such times, is an almost wholly symbolic activity, and to see the pluck and twitch of your line in the current is to know a very particular anticipation. That somehow, in the connection with the invisible forms below, you'll connect with your own deep history.

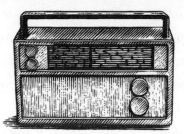

TWO

THE YEAR IS 1961, IT'S A SULTRY DAY IN EARLY SEPTEMBER, and I'm seven. In a couple of days' time I start at boarding school, a thought that induces an empty chill behind my breastbone. It's ordained, however, and the process is no more to be resisted than the summer's end. New pyjamas have been bought, new face flannels and Chilprufe vests have been name-taped, new football boots wait in their box. 'You must be excited,' people say, and I gravely agree that this is the case.

For the moment, though, summer is hanging on, stale and a little desperate, and my parents have driven me and my brothers Anthony and James to Swanbourne Lake, four miles from where we live in West Sussex. It's a pretty spot, lying in the wooded lee of Arundel Castle, but it's crowded. There are busy queues at the tea caravan and the ice-cream stall, and wasps are swirling around the overflowing litterbins. At the lakeside, you can hire rowing boats from a weather-beaten couple in brown coats. The couple have a small hut, in front of which is a chair with a transistor radio on it, playing 'Fings Ain't What They Used to Be', by Max Bygraves. The radio, a newish model, has attracted a circle of mostly male admirers, and in the tea queue women in floppy sunhats are laughing and swaying along to the chorus.

My brothers and I are interested spectators of this bonhomie, while my parents watch with rather more detachment. My father is in his shirtsleeves and his flannel trousers are held up with a regimental tie. My mother is in a straw hat and an Italian print dress. Neither has embraced the concept of 'leisure' clothing, nor ever will. Until the day that he dies, my father will never wear any form of T-shirt, untailored jacket, or shoe without laces. He simply wouldn't have been capable of it, any more than my mother would have been capable of wearing slacks or of dyeing her hair.

As there's a bit of a wait for the boats, we join the ice-cream queue, and are eventually face to face with the gypsyish stall-owner and her rocker son, who glares at us with surly contempt from beneath his oily quiff as he hands us our ice creams, which come in round moulded wafers called oysters. Finally, with an hour's hire paid, we push off from the bank in one of the heavy, clinker-built skiffs. Recoated each spring with green lead paint, these are built to withstand daily collisions and are powered by massive oars in clanking rowlocks. Slowly, to my father's steady pull, we move away from the shore.

For a time Anthony and I return to one of our favourite

meditations, which concerns the poisoning of one of his school-mates. If he dies, runs our reasoning, then we will not have to go to another of his birthday parties: overpoweringly melancholy events featuring warm orange barley water, Shippam's paste sandwiches and organized games. A generous cocktail of yew, foxglove, jack-in-the-pulpit and deadly nightshade should do it – like all country children, we know which plants and berries are the most toxic – but that's the easy bit. The harder part will be persuading our victim to swallow the mixture and then preventing him from shopping us to his parents while in his death throes. In some ways, we agree, it probably makes more sense to wipe out the entire family.

These musings, while constituting a comforting retreading of old ground, fail to dispel my growing sense of apprehension, or the feeling that something irrecoverable is about to come to an end. In less than thirty-six hours' time I will be lying in bed in a dormitory full of total strangers. Trailing my fingers over the side of the boat, I stare into the water. We are at the far end of the lake from the crowds now, sliding through the clear water in the shadow of a stand of trees. At intervals shafts of refracted sunlight pierce the branches and the looking-glass surface, illuminating the emerald weed six feet below, like the canopy of a tropical forest. I'm staring down into one such column of light when suddenly the greenery parts and a large eel glides into view. For a moment I see it clearly – the arrow-taper of the head, the fanning pectorals, the muscular grace of the bronze body – and then it's gone.

I stare after it into the olive shadows. 'I saw an eel!' I say, and the others lunge for the side of the boat, sending the shadows rocking. What I can't explain is that it's not just the eel, it's the revelation – the opening and closing of the shutter on an alien world. That tall, mysterious chamber of green, speared with light but vanishing into darkness. What Aztec empires might that darkness hold? What escape might it represent?

THREE

My first rod came from a tobacconist in Arundel High Street – an impulse buy by my father, who had gone in for a packet of Senior Service. It was about five feet long and made of fibreglass, with a wooden handle and an alloy reel-seat kept in place with a nail. It came with a two-inch, centre-pin reel that had been enamelled a weird pink colour, a packet of hooks and split-shot, a float, and twenty yards of bright-green line. I was eight.

When my father brought it back to the car I insisted on trying it out immediately. We drove out of town until we came to a place where a stream ran under the road. I laboriously rigged up the whole thing, lashing the hook to the line with a sturdy quadruple granny knot. A hurried roadside search revealed a fat earthworm. Attaching this to the hook, I pulled the line off the reel, which screamed in protest, and swung the tackle into the water a yard in front of me. To my delight the float cocked. Three feet below it I could see the worm wriggling on its hook. Grasping the rod handle with both hands I waited for a fish to dash out and take it – an event which, surely, could be only seconds away. Minutes passed, but nothing happened. The bait just hung there below me. No fish came. And yet surely I was doing everything right? Surely there could be no more to it than this? I looked round at my father, who shrugged philosophically and lit another Senior Service. Half an hour later, by unspoken mutual consent, we gave up.

It would be seven years before I caught anything on that rod. Although essentially a toy and horribly constructed, it was the perfect size for brook fishing. We had moved from Sussex by then, to a rainswept corner of Powys. Our roof leaked, but the place was beautiful and for a young fisherman it was paradise. In every direction were bracken-covered hills intercut with tumbling rock streams. If you crept uphill on hands and knees, hauling yourself up the boulders and pushing between the ferns, you could flick a worm into every tiny pool and, as often as not, see a trout race out from beneath some mossy overhang to grab it.

That, however, was far in the future, and in those Sussex days I had no one to get me started. No one in my family fished or, as far as I could discover, had ever fished, for generations back. My grandfather, then in his late eighties, claimed that as a young man, before the First World War, he had once accidentally scooped a large bream into a rowing boat with an oar, but was forced to admit that he'd had no contact with live fish since that occasion.

So I learnt from books. In the school holidays I took the number 66 bus to Arundel, walked up the hill to the public library on Maltravers Street and one by one took out every book they had on fishing. And as it happened they had the best. Bernard Venables, Richard Walker, Peter Stone, Fred Taylor – all of the titans were there. The 1960s were a golden age of angling writing, and these men, who all knew each other well, and often fished together, were the pioneers of many of the methods now regarded as standard.

Bernard Venables was the poet of the group, and his definitive work, published in 1953 and simply entitled *Fishing*, is one of the most elegiac books written on any sport. No one loved the technical business of angling more than Venables, or was happier than when immersing himself in the minutiae of float design or shotting patterns, but his real subject was England and Englishness. Here he is on fishing for trout in the Thames:

A little before the time, which will often be in the evening, [the angler] will be there, ready for his chance. This is a transient but immortal piece of time: the sun will have fallen behind the mantled downs, the air will be heavy with that evening scent of water that can conjure a sort of madness in the fisherman. A smell is not an easy thing to carry in the memory, but an angler exiled anywhere can recall it from the fabric of his mind and

in a moment be enraptured. The water will be dark now,
purple and dusky cobalt, richly green and amber in the
shallows, the clots of foam will be turned to blue…
Moments are hours, the bark of a distant dog hardly
noticed at the time, will be found afterwards to be
lodged immovable in the memory.

Richard Walker, possibly the most visionary angler England
has produced, was also the most beguiling of teachers, seamlessly
interweaving atmospheric anecdote and hard-core instruction.
You stood beside him on the bank, free-lining a flake of crust to
shadowy chub in a willow pool, or watching as your roach live-
bait was engulfed by a huge pike, leaving only a shower of silvery
scales. Peter Stone, meanwhile, was the affable pragmatist, the
sort of bloke you might get talking to in a pub, who would
draw you a diagram of a fast-water barbel rig on the back of a
beer mat. And 'Fred J', as he was always known, was the genial
humorist, constantly bantering with his sidemen, brother Ken
and cousin Joe, and loosing a ripe stream of 'unparliamentary
language' when a big one got away.

Which, it has to be said, wasn't often. There were others who
didn't write fishing books but featured in all of them, specimen
hunters and angling theorists like Maurice Ingham and Pete
Thomas. For young anglers of my generation, these quiet, dedicated countrymen were our spirit guides. I had no idea beyond

the odd black-and-white photograph what any of them looked like, but I felt I knew them, and when years later I fished waters that they had made famous, like the Royalty on the Hampshire Avon, I sensed their presence there.

I owe so much to that unnamed but enlightened book-buyer at Arundel library – surely an angler himself. I remember Peter Stone's *Legering* arriving there. It was published in 1963 and the library bought it the following year, when I was eleven. To my enormous satisfaction I was the first to take it out, newly wrapped in its clear plastic jacket. Recently I looked through the used book lists on the internet to see whether I could find a copy. There was one, a first edition heart-stoppingly marked 'library copy', which had found its way to a store in Chicago, Illinois, and now cost over $200.

I tended to borrow books and run, because browsing in the library meant that one was likely to come to the notice of Mr Fox. 'Firefighter' Fox was a master at my school. A dapper Scotsman in the autumn of his life, he had at some point suffered a severe head injury that had left him with a matchbox-sized indentation in his forehead and a wild-eyed, eccentric manner. At some point in his career, according to rumour, he had also served with the local fire service, hence his nickname.

Whilst this colourful background did not make Firefighter a compelling English teacher, he was nevertheless a generally benign bloke with two obsessions that could be counted on to enliven a class. The first of these, which was not unreasonable given that he was a devout Catholic and a loyal Scot, was a visceral hatred of Queen Elizabeth I. The second, rather more obscure, was his unswerving admiration for László Bíró, the Hungarian-born inventor of the ballpoint pen. An extreme pedant in matters of pronunciation, Firefighter insisted that biro should be pronounced *beer-oh*, and that any deviation from this, particularly *byre-oh*, represented a slur against the great man. To either of these topics, he would rise like a starving trout, never learning from experience.

PUPIL (*looking up innocently from* Dragon Book of Verse):
Excuse me, sir, why was Elizabeth I called the Virgin
Queen?
Fox (*bristling*): The *Virgin* Queen? To all right-thinking
men she was the Bastard Queen.
PUPIL: Oh, come on, sir. At least she executed Mary
Queen of Scots.
SECOND PUPIL (*as Fox's eyes begin to bulge*): Sir, please Sir,
my pen's run out. Can I borrow a biro?

And so on.

Fox haunted the Arundel library. It was no more than a couple of hundred yards from the cathedral, and whenever the bells rang out, as they did at least four times hourly, he would sink to his knees in a quasi-mediaeval display of piety. If I happened to be there, he would forcibly compel me to do the same thing. Given the library's popularity, this was more than a little embarrassing. I remember roomfuls of respectable browsers staring at the pair of us open-mouthed: Firefighter kneeling in prayer, his lips moving slowly, his hand heavy on my shoulder, and me bowed in mortification over a copy of Peter Stone's *Bream and Barbel*.

I read, and from working my way through the key angling texts as voraciously as a pike through a tank of goldfish, I amassed a huge backlog of theory on subjects like free-lining, long-trotting and stret-pegging, the use of the slider float and the paternoster rig, the application of the Arlesey bomb and the coffin-lead. One of the few books I actually owned was *Teach Yourself Fishing* by Tom Rodway. There were Teach Yourself books on every conceivable subject, from Swahili to stamp collecting, trigonometry to personal efficiency. They cost five shillings, came in a distinctive blue-and-yellow hardback cover and were small enough to jam into a school trouser pocket. *Teach Yourself Fishing*, which covered every aspect of the sport, was practical without being too specialist and, because it didn't have to be returned to the library, could be kept at my side during term-time. With the help of a torch, its discussions of hook sizes, shotting patterns and monofilament breaking-strains could be pored over under the sheets in the dormitory after lights-out (batteries had shorter lives in those days, but you could buy yourself extra reading time by leaving them on a warm radiator during the day).

Rodway's instructions and black-and-white line drawings would transport me to realms I knew from my reading but had never visited. In my imagination I slipped through the Norfolk Broads in a flat-bottomed punt, amassing huge catches of roach and bream. I cast subtly prepared baits to monstrous carp in elm-fringed Hertfordshire ponds at nightfall, watched the give-away needle bubbles of tench on Blenheim Palace lake at dawn, saw the ranunculus streamers on the Hampshire Avon part to reveal magisterial ranks of feeding barbel and chub.

And as each leviathan was hooked, landed and gently returned, there would be a nod of approval from the spirit guides. From Richard Walker in his battered felt hat, from the genially chuckling Fred J, or from Mr Crabtree, quietly tamping his pipe. Mr Crabtree was the fictional star of a comic strip in the *Daily Mirror*, drawn by Bernard Venables. Originally created to dispense horticultural advice, Mr Crabtree found fame when, one winter's day when there was nothing much to do in the garden, Venables had him go fishing. The response from the public was immediate. Seeing which way the wind was blowing, the *Mirror* allowed Venables to phase out the hardy perennials.

The collected comic strips, published as *Mr Crabtree Goes Fishing*, became the best-selling angling book of the twentieth century. In each strip the sapient Crabtree takes his ten-year-old son Peter fishing. There is infinite time for this, and wherever the pair go – willow-shaded chalk streams, slack-water pike swims, reed-fringed lakes full of specimen tench – they always have the place to themselves. When they go live-baiting for pike, Mr Crabtree introduces Peter to 'Tom, the bait-catcher', a deferential figure in a flat cap. And of course, in this unchanging dream world, they never have a blank day. Sooner or later the quill float shudders or the live-bait is seized, and after a short but dramatic battle Peter is marvelling over yet another prize. In all of this, every nuance of weather and water is realized in black-and-white line illustration. And yet it was not implausible, nor was Mr Crabtree an improbable figure. There were elements of him in my father and in the fathers of my school friends: trilby-wearing, pipe-smoking professional men who had fought in the Second World War and then returned to the British countryside.

It was a conflict that, in the early 1960s, was still very much in the schoolboy consciousness. Without exception, we read War Picture Library comics, played with 8th Army and Afrika Korps mini-soldiers, made Airfix models of Spitfires and Lancaster bombers, owned Luger cap-guns, and watched films like *Albert RN* and *I Was Monty's Double*. And of course the games we organized in our free time were always British versus German. The rules were straightforward. A bramble patch in the school grounds represented a fort that had to be taken or defended. Both sides would pile in, wrestling opponents to the ground and riddling them with fire from invisible Tommy guns and Schmeissers. Inevitably, the line between history and imagination became blurred. One school friend, born as I was in 1953, breezily confided to the rest of the class that although he preferred not to talk about it, both his parents had actually been tortured to death by the Nazis. At seven years of age, we saw no reason to disbelieve him.

Mr Crabtree, I imagined, had been an officer in one of the more technical regiments, the REME, perhaps, or the Royal Engineers. And he had then gone on to manage a local auctioneers, maybe, or work in a land agency, thus making the connections that provided access to so many miles of fishing. Peter's mother, whom we never meet but who spends happy days preparing steamed pike with parsley sauce, might well have been a Wren. And their cook-housekeeper Patsy, to whose reddened hands are consigned more mundane tasks like roasting perch and ironing Peter's shorts, had probably worked in a munitions factory.

Although jeans became popular for children in the 1960s, many mothers, learning the hard way what a nightmare they were to wash by hand, and how resistant to the mangle, kept their sons in shorts for as much of the year as possible. The result, for middle-class country boys like me, was perpetually bramble-scratched legs and scabbed knees, with the resultant scars worn as a badge of pride. Peter Crabtree never wears anything except shorts, just as his father, whatever the circumstances, is never without a tie.

The biographer Adam Sisman, a one-time fishing companion

of the poet Ted Hughes, once elaborated an entire Crabtree mythos to me, in which Mr Crabtree became a policeman after the war and was involved in the 1967 drugs bust of The Rolling Stones. The *Daily Mirror* strip was launched just after the war, but outside London the slow-moving, socially conservative world it described was still very much in place two decades later – certainly in our corner of West Sussex. When he was six, my brother Anthony asked his English teacher who The Beatles were. 'They're four very wicked young men,' came the answer, and there the matter rested.

Thanks to the library, I soon had angling theory to spare. What I needed, badly, was practice. This, however, was less straightforward than it might have been, as there were very few fishable places within bus or bicycle-riding range. At once the most accessible and the least promising was the village duck pond, a shallow and dispiriting body of water with an ornamental island in the middle bearing a single dwarf willow. It was bordered on three sides by roads and on the fourth by a melancholy parade of shops, including one selling only knitting wool. You occasionally saw boys fishing the pond, but you never, ever saw anyone catch anything. I must have tried it a dozen times over the years without getting so much as a bite. I tried bread, worms, maggots – all the usual baits. Nothing. A couple of times I threw spinners out, on the off chance that all the other fish had been devoured by a monster pike. Nothing again. And for once, the books were no help. Wide as they cast their net, Richard Walker and Peter Stone didn't have much to say about duck ponds.

The second possibility was the river. The Arun at Arundel, four miles from our house, was huge and sluggish. Tidal for miles inland, its water was an impenetrable grey, whilst its banks were greasy, gumboot-swallowing ramparts of mud and olive slime. Having tried it a few times, my friend Paul and I eventually gave up, defeated. Floats and baits would be hurtled downstream by the current, while leger-rigs would immediately snag up in the rocky mud-soup of the river bed. We weren't using heavy enough tackle, of course, but it would have been a challenging venue even if we were. The height and slipperiness of the banks made fishing dangerous as well as difficult, and the whole thing was rendered even harder by the safety equipment that my father insisted that we take with us. Life jackets might have made sense, yet he settled on fifty yards of rope and a marine anchor. Exactly what we were supposed to do with these we never quite worked out, although just dragging them from the bus to the water's edge half killed us. We were desperate to fish, but this was no fun whatsoever.

The third and by far the most promising local water was the 'weed pond'. Owned by a farmer and no more than a quarter-acre in size, it abutted a side road half a mile from our house, and was surrounded on the other three sides by cornfields. Its margins were overgrown and its surface almost completely choked with lily pads and floating pondweed. However, there was a jagged crack of black water under some trees where, in theory, you could crouch down and swing out a baited line. And if you waited under the elder bushes on a hot summer afternoon, and the light was right, you could just see shadowy forms nosing amongst the lily stems. Real fish, just like in the books, and just a few yards away. How difficult could they be to catch?

The answer, I quickly discovered, was very difficult indeed. The first problem was getting into position. You had to make your approach from behind a rusted barn, crawl under a barbed-wire fence and proceed on all fours through a thicket of cow parsley, flowering bramble and mature nettles. Hunkering on the narrow bank with the sun behind you, your knees and the backs of your hands prickling from the nettles, and the midges swarming around your face, you looked out over the pond, its surface covered in a thin scum of verdigris-coloured weed. About fifteen feet in front of you a ragged break in the green broadened to a darkly inviting pool perhaps three feet across. Were the fish still there, or had you spooked them? A single heavy footfall or a rod shadow waving over the water would have seen them fade like ghosts. The answer was almost always the same: the fish were gone, and the pool had the opaque, faintly disturbed look that signals failure.

Occasionally, just occasionally, I was stealthy enough to make it into position undetected. And as I crouched there with my heart pounding, my feet hot in my plimsolls and the thick scent of cow parsley in my nose, I could see the tell-tale tremor at the edge of the weeds, the faint shifting of shadows, the dimpling as invisible morsels were drawn from the surface film into probing, cartilaginous mouths. These were good fish – roach or rudd I guessed, and perhaps a few crucian carp – and some of them could well be around the pound mark. To catch one of these magic creatures and to hold it shimmering in my hands would be... I couldn't imagine what it would be like. It would be to enter another realm of existence altogether.

But seeing was one thing and catching another. To get a bait out to the fish meant a fifteen-foot cast of pinpoint accuracy through an obstacle course of overhanging snags. I wasn't by any means the only one after these fish, as at least a dozen snapped-off tangles of line in the branches attested. Half the boys in the village had them in their sights, and it was their efforts that had educated the fish to such an extreme pitch of caution. Even if I were to avoid the snags, a splashy cast would send my quarry racing into cover.

In the event, the same scenario played itself out again and again. I'd gingerly swing the bait out with an underarm cast and it would fall several feet short. I would then be faced with the choice: do I leave it where it is – in the wrong place but at least in the water – or try again and risk a snag? I'd always go for the second choice. Out would go the bait, this time with a bit more force. And then, invariably, a horrible silence. No watery plop, no jaunty cocking of the quill float, just the tackle swinging disconsolately from the overhanging foliage.

For a moment I'd put off admitting to myself that this had happened. I'd give the line the softest of pulls, to try to dislodge the hook. This never worked – it just drove the hook deeper into the branch. So I'd pull harder. Possibly, just possibly, the branch could be snapped off. But it was summer and the wood was green. So I'd pull again, really hard this time, which would achieve nothing except to send the shadow of the branch skittering across the surface and scatter any remaining fish once and for all. Angry now, knowing that it was all over, I'd point the rod at the snag and reel the line tight. Soon the nylon monofilament would be humming with tension while the offending bough twitched under the strain, shedding insects and fragments of twig into the water below. Another couple of ratchet clicks and the line would part with a crack like a pistol shot. Glumly, knowing the session was over, I'd wade out into the muddy water to retrieve my hook and float, and then, plimsolls squelching, start the half-mile trudge home.

On a couple of occasions, by some miracle of co-ordination and good luck, I managed to send my baited hook careening between the overhanging branches to land on target. Sadly, however, that was where the story ended. My bread pellet would hang there untouched – a dim, pale speck two feet beneath the surface – for as many hours as I stayed there. The fish, meanwhile, were cheerfully feeding away on the far side of the pond. The moment I packed up, of course, they'd be back again, dimpling and nosing and carrying on as if the previous few hours had never happened.

They drove me crazy, those fish. I hated them for the effortlessness with which they evaded me, and I hated myself for my heavy-handed incompetence. The trouble was that I was ten years old and impatient in all things. When you made an Airfix model of a Spitfire, the prevailing wisdom (at our school, at least) was that you were supposed to paint the various parts first with enamel paint – brown and green camouflage on top, duck-egg blue below – and only when this was dry could you glue the whole thing together. One way and another, it was at least a forty-eight-hour process. But I could never bear to wait. I wanted the completed plane immediately, so I'd glue all the parts together at high speed and then, with the thing still wobbly on its wheels, start painting. The results were as messy as may be imagined and never good enough to hang on a thread from the ceiling. On the positive side, though, these exercises left me with a very satisfactory carapace of dried Airfix glue all over my fingers. This resolutely resisted the school Lifebuoy soap and would remain on the fingers until picked off flake by flake – the perfect way to spend a slow-moving maths or geography class.

Two things distinguished the really well-made model Spitfire: the propeller whizzed round satisfyingly when you blew on it, and you could see the pilot in the cockpit. To get the propeller to go round, you had to assemble it, let the glue dry for twenty-four hours, and then slot it into place as you joined the two halves of the fuselage. In order to see the pilot, you had to apply the finest filament of Airfix glue to the cockpit surround and snap the canopy delicately into place. If you were clumsy, and got the powerful solvent on the transparent plastic, as I invariably did, it would corrode, bubbling into an opaque froth.

Real Spitfire canopies looked a bit like this, I discovered later, if the main header tank was hit by enemy cannon-fire. The tank was located directly in front of the cockpit, and the high-octane fuel would ignite with ferocious speed, melting the canopy and drowning the pilot in a torrent of flame. My father got to know a number of fighter pilots who had suffered this fate after he himself had been severely burnt in a tank battle shortly after D-Day. With his situation critical, he was flown home to the pioneering reconstructive unit in East Grinstead run by the plastic surgeon Archibald McIndoe. There, after more than forty agonizing operations, he became a member of the exclusive Guinea Pig Club, made up of the servicemen who had been in the care of McIndoe and his burns team.

The Guinea Pigs were a drinking club, and given the hell that they'd endured – the months of pain, the constant stench of open wounds and putrefying flesh, the screams that echoed through the wards every night as the nightmares returned, the fear that the outside world would find their rebuilt faces freakish and grotesque – these young men had earned the right to take a drink or two. However dark the hour, most of them managed to hold on to their sense of humour. There were macabre practical jokes. Patients recovering consciousness after operations, for example, would wake to find themselves rouged and lipsticked like prostitutes, or laid out like corpses with funereal wreaths on their chests. My father was one of the luckier ones, in that his face eventually healed well. You'd have known that he'd been badly burnt at some point, but that was the limit of it. The lasting damage was to his hands. His fingers never straightened, and the joints were stiff and painful for the rest of his life.

After that first day, when I was eight, he never fished with me again. Even if he'd been interested in it, which he wasn't, the intricate businesses of knot tying and hook handling would have been beyond him. He encouraged me from a distance, though, looking up from his desk or his book with a solicitous 'Any luck?' when I returned at the end of a session, to which the answer was invariably a mute shake of the head. This detached approach suited us both. There were areas in which he could still be my guide, but this was not one of them. I had to make the journey alone.

FOUR

By my eleventh birthday I still hadn't actually caught a fish and was beginning to doubt that I ever would. It never occurred to me that there was any course open to me other than bashing on by myself. Had my father known more about the fishing scene, he might have directed me to a local club, most of which ran junior sections and where I might have learnt some practical technique. But he didn't, probably assuming that, if left to my own devices, I'd get there in the end. Which I did – in the end.

The winter of 1965 was a dour one, and on a cold and misty Saturday morning shortly after the beginning of the spring term the whole school was summoned to watch Winston Churchill's funeral on television. Knowing very well who Churchill was and what he had saved us from, we sat in silent, cross-legged rows while the ceremony unfolded. As the cranes in the London docks dipped in respect as the funeral barge passed by, the nebulous outlines on the small black-and-white screen and the sombre mood of the occasion seemed to fuse.

Winters were long, in those days, and school light bulbs feeble. From the beginning of the September term to the end of the Easter holidays in May, we passed our waking hours in an autumnal half-light. We didn't resent this; on the contrary, we welcomed the privacy and sense of enclosure that it afforded us. We were natural whisperers and plotters in corners, constantly fired by intrigue, rumour and speculation. The school itself, a warren of backstair passages, creaking corridors and ambiguous, dark-panelled rooms, encouraged us in this course. Cabals would suddenly crystallize around a single activity – table-turning seances, the experimental smoking of crushed maple leaves, the swapping of Rolling Stones memorabilia or back copies of *Parade* magazine – and equally suddenly dissolve as secrecy was compromised.

It snowed most years. The most memorable freeze was in the winter of 1962–3. The autumn had been cold; on Christmas Day the skies were battleship grey, and on Boxing Day the snow came racing in. For twenty-four hours blizzard followed blizzard, and when we finally ventured outside, the world was a glaring, hard-edged white. The snow settled, layer after frozen layer, and soon a pattern began to establish itself. Mornings and early afternoons were generally clear, perfect for tracking foxes and sledging down the precipitous slope of the dell at the side of the drive. At tea-time, as the light began to fail, we'd retreat inside, kicking off our boots and exchanging the blue-white dazzle we'd left behind for the yellow wash of the wall sconces and parchment-shaded lamps of my father's study. Beyond the faded damask curtains, meanwhile, flakes would begin to fall again, beating soundlessly at the windows and whirling the lawns and fields into invisibility.

By the beginning of the January term so many roads were impassable that the school could not reopen – a thrilling and appalling contravention of the natural order. Every morning I woke expecting to see a thaw, but every night brought a fresh fall. In the fields, the snow was now waist-deep. In the drifts at the edge of the woods, it was taller than I was. Time, for those weeks, stood still, and comparisons were drawn with the great winter of 1947, a quarter of a century earlier. I had seen plenty of snow in my nine years, but nothing as life-transforming as this.

One effect of the freeze was that a hard carapace would form over evergreen trees and bushes so that if you distributed your weight carefully, you could climb up and over them. A short walk from the house there was a wood – dark even in summer – whose dense, overgrown laurels were so thickly blanketed with frozen snow that I was able to crawl from treetop to treetop. It was heart-stoppingly exciting, and at first, fearful of falling through the frozen canopy, I inched along on my belly. I soon discovered, though, that I was safer moving at speed, shimmying across the traverses in a series of dashes.

The roof of the wood was another world, a place of immaculate formations, glittering white dunes, implacable steel skies. I spent hours up there, imagining myself in some long-lost Arctic kingdom, or on an extra-galactic ice planet where all communication was by telepathy. It was a world that I could only have discovered as a skinny child; with another year's worth of flesh on my bones I'd have been too heavy to climb those snowy ramparts. And while descent was a thrill – pulling the tails of my plastic mac between my legs and scooting down on my backside into a six-foot drift – I was always sad to leave. When the thaw came, as some day soon it must, I knew that there would be no return to those sparkling heights.

It was the winter to end all winters, as lethal to many as it was magical to me, and in retrospect it's hard not to see it as a final rallying of nature's forces against the onslaught of post-war capitalism. Against fields drenched in insecticide, rivers saturated with chemical run-off, mediaeval hedgerows stripped out by rapacious agri-businesses, thousand-year-old woods felled by property developers. It was the expiring cry of Morgan le Fay, and the winters that followed had a sullen, defeated quality to them. It would snow again, in later years, but with nothing like the ferocity of that winter.

At some point in the summer term following the Churchill funeral, my father announced that we would be spending several weeks of the holidays in Shropshire, where he had rented a country house. This was a popular arrangement in the 1960s and, although lavish-sounding, actually a much less expensive option for a family holiday than one involving flights, restaurants and hotels. As the arrangements were often cash-based, there were bargains to be had. Impoverished aristocrats, in particular, didn't want their houses lingering embarrassingly in the To Let column of *The Times*, where they and their owners might be identified. What accommodation my father arrived at with the owner of this particular house, I don't know, and I certainly wasn't interested at the time. One fact, dropped casually but significantly into his description of the place, occupied my mind to the exclusion of all else. 'There's a lake,' he told me. 'A lake you can fish in.'

Could this really be true? Surely, when we got there, the 'lake' would turn out to be a glorified water feature, or an unusually wet marsh. Or if a proper lake, it would be entirely void of fish, like the Walberton duck pond. That it could possibly be the real thing, and that I would have unlimited access to it, seemed just too much to hope for. I decided to count on nothing. To wait and see.

The term dragged its feet, as summer terms do, but finally ended. The beginning of the holidays was taken up with an orgy of packing: metal trunks, field stoves, reserves of tinned food, candles in case of power cuts, groundsheets, calamine, sunhats, wound dressings, suturing equipment and long-expired antibiotics. My mother, an enthusiastic amateur physician who had once run a Cub Scout troop, planned for holidays as if for a war.

Finally, after a long, rattling drive in our battered grey Bedford van, with no more than a couple of stops for roadside vomiting – the combination of my father's pipe smoke and the sideways benches in the back of the van tended to make these an inevitability – we arrived in Shropshire.

This was a very different landscape from that of chalky, flinty, commuter-belt West Sussex, where it always felt as if the sea was just a few fields away. Shropshire had the wild contours of the border counties – the dark ridge of the Long Mynd, the green escarpment of Wenlock Edge – but there was a voluptuousness there too, a softness to the curve of the limestone hills and a beery brightness to the rivers that spoke of something less austere. Of pouring sunshine, pollen-heavy air, and fields drowsy with bees and clover.

The house didn't trouble to advertise itself to the outside world. A discreet exit from a minor road was followed by a long drive between cornfields, past a walled garden and down an alleé of rose bushes. These led, quite suddenly, into a shadowed courtyard, from which reared castellated grey walls spotted with yellow lichen. Inside the house was cool and stone-floored. As I stepped through the front door, avoiding a rope-handled box containing a Jacques croquet set, I was met by the faint, biscuity smell of old furniture and gun oil. In front of me was a high-ceilinged hall hung with Civil War armour, engraved maps of the estate, hunting crops, antlers, foxes' masks and gymkhana rosettes. There were also – and my eyes fixed on these before all else – several rod racks, bearing fully made-up cane rods. These were long – three sections each, at least – with brass ferrules and dark-varnished bindings, and were clearly in regular use. From each cork handle hung a well-maintained centre-pin reel. An Aerial or Star-Back, loaded with greenish monofilament line.

I stared, open-mouthed. I'd never been into a house where kit was laid out like this, ready to be taken down and used at a moment's notice. Where fishing was considered part of everyday life, rather than an exotic and even perverse pursuit. The house had other wonders – portraits by Romney and Reynolds, Chippendale furniture, curtained four-poster beds – but these, for the moment, didn't interest me. Following an instinctive course through half-darkened rooms, I made for the garden door.

Outside, as a last golden intensity of light announced the onset of evening, the ground fell away in a series of gentle terraces linked by lichened flights of steps. Beyond the garden were the thousand acres of the estate, a green and gold patchwork of cornfields, woods and coppices that seemed to gather itself skywards as it approached the horizon. The lake, one end just visible, was a dark gleam at the bottom of the valley. And for the next three weeks all this was mine.

FIVE

As soon as I'd had breakfast the next morning, I went to see the gardener, who lived in one of the cottages.

'Speak to Tom about the fishing,' the owner had told my father. 'He'll tell your boy where to go and what to do.'

Tom was in his late fifties, with weathered features, tousled hair and a roll-up permanently positioned between his lips. He gave me a friendly grin, nodded and led me to the dim, loam-scented outhouse where he kept his fishing tackle. In a corner was a sack full of sphagnum moss and red brandling worms. Taking a generous handful of these, he dropped them into a jam jar, screwed on the lid, which was ventilated with air holes, and lifted his rod from the wall. It was fully made up.

'Ready?' he asked.

I followed him across the courtyard and down the steps at the front of the house. The sun had burnt the dew from the grass and there was not so much as a whisper of breeze. Tom glanced at my tackle. The green horror had been replaced by my eleventh-birthday present, a fibreglass spinning-rod seven feet six inches long with a decent cork grip, an uplocking reel-seat and a test curve of about a pound and a quarter, bought from Russell Hillsdon Sports of Chichester. There's no such thing as an all-purpose boy's rod, but if there were, it would have been that one. The pink reel had quickly fallen to bits. Its place was now taken by a proper centre-pin, a copy of a Westley-Richards Speedia in shiny pressed alloy that I'd bought with saved-up pocket money from the tobacconist in Arundel. The canvas bag over my shoulder – from Hardy's of Pall Mall, no less, a gift from my godmother whose husband's aristocratic aunt owned a rather grand stretch of the Eden in Cumbria – held a modest selection of hooks, floats and weights from Woolworth's and a bait-box I'd made by repeatedly jabbing the point of a compass through the lid of a pipe-tobacco tin discarded by a geography teacher at school. (This individual, a part-time scoutmaster who'd spent several years 'knocking about the Middle East', was always preceded by the chocolatey fumes of the Erinmore Flake that he smoked. Towards the end of our prep school years he would conceive a hopeless devotion for my friend Jamie and, casting around for a suitable way of expressing his feelings, sign him up for a year's subscription to the *Reader's Digest*. Jamie's parents were, to say the least, bemused.)

'Done much fishing?' Tom asked quietly, as we made our way between grazing cattle.

I looked down at the lake. The end nearest us was open and shallow, fringed by reeds. The far end was darker and deeper, masked by trees.

'Not that much,' I said.

He took me to the shallow end. From the dry trodden mud it was clear that this was where the cattle came to drink. The water was a semi-transparent olive, unruffled by the faintest breeze. Sitting down on a hummock, Tom watched and smoked as I fumblingly assembled my rod, slid a red cork float up the line, nipped on a couple of split-shot with my teeth, and jabbed my Size 12 hook through an angrily wriggling brandling.

I cast, surreptitiously putting all the beef into it I could muster. There was a whistling sound and my end-tackle nearly took Tom's eye out before landing with an ugly splash about ten feet away. Tom grinned but said nothing. Example, rather than spoken instruction, was his way. Lifting his own rod, he gave it the gentlest of underarm swings and sent his tackle looping soundlessly into deep water. Just a few minutes later his quill float began to twitch, then slid underwater. The rod-tip kicked and juddered as he drew a six-inch perch to the side and lifted it into the air for unhooking. I stared, mesmerized, at its amber eyes and scarlet fins as it lay on the cracked brown palm of his hand.

'A good friend to the fisherman is the perch,' Tom observed quietly, watching it swim off in a puff of disturbed mud.

I recast, a little more calmly this time. Minutes passed, and this time it was my float that began to shudder. 'Wait for him,' counselled Tom. I did so, my heart pounding, and a few moments later my float slid confidently underwater. I struck.

Walker, Crabtree and the other spirit guides all have much to say on the subject of the strike. Most speak of a quick, decisive flick of the wrist to hook the fish in the lip before it swallows the bait or spits it out. I struck so hard that the fish rocketed into the air above our heads and landed behind me.

'I think you have him,' murmured Tom dryly, as I laid down my rod and followed my line through the warm grass. At the top of the bank flapped a seven-inch perch, its armoured flanks shimmering and its translucent dorsal fin bristling in half-stunned defiance.

Looking back, the sight of that little predator gasping out its life in the grass was a pitiful one. But I had different eyes then, and those were different times. For the event and my own fierce satisfaction to be complete, the fish had to be killed, displayed and, as a conclusion, eaten. Only then would the ritual – my private initiation – have meaning.

Tom seemed to understand this without anything having to be said, and showed me how to put a thumb into the fish's mouth and twist back to break its neck. When it was over, I looked down at the small, still form and watched the silver-blue flush fade from its flanks. Dead, it somehow looked even more elemental, as if it had been fashioned from the olive-brown water in which it had lived.

I think that part of me knew, even at eleven, that killing the fish – reducing it to an object that could be stared at and manhandled – had not solved its mystery. I had read Roger Lancelyn Green's schoolboy digest of the *Iliad* and was uneasily familiar with Achilles' gloating over the corpse of Hector. Nonetheless, the greater part of me simply felt triumph. I was a hunter, an outwitter of wild creatures, and here was the proof of my skill. It was, to a degree, expected of me.

In those days people still had specimen fish mounted by taxidermists, and in country pubs or hotels you'd often come face to face with a vast pike or chalk-stream trout in a bow-fronted glass case. They had a solemn power, those cased fish, which never failed to stop me in my tracks. There was usually a spray of varnished reeds, a faded blue background, and a gilt-painted legend: *Brown trout, 9 lb 8 oz, caught by Col. J. Wickham, Longparish, 9th June 1938.*

For all their atmospheric power, however, these varnished and glassy-eyed specimens told you no more about the mystery of the original wild creature than a balding tiger-skin rug tells you about the reality of the tiger. And there was often something melancholy about such pharaonic attempts to suspend time. If the decay of the brown trout, nine pounds eight ounces, had been arrested, and if some vestige of the original remained with us still, it was hard to believe that this was true of Colonal J. Wickham. What were the details of that golden day on the Test? To whom did the colonel bear back, in breathless triumph, the catch of a lifetime? We will never know, any more than we will ever learn the circumstances that led, a couple of decades later, to the sale of his trophy as part of a dusty job lot of 'curios' at some suburban auction house.

I caught several fish that first day on the lake, and many more in the weeks that followed. I ate my perch, as well as several of its larger cousins, and learnt what the French have long known: that fried in butter with a sprig of fresh parsley it is the subtlest-tasting of freshwater fish. And I began, finally, to learn the art of angling. Every few days Tom would accompany me over the dewy morning fields, showing me new places and how to approach them silently, how to pre-bait a swim, how to recognize the needle bubbles that indicate feeding tench, how to present a pinch of breadflake to nervous roach, how to tell whether there was a big perch or pike around. Not that he put a great deal of this into words; he just did as he'd always done, and I copied him.

Today's high-tech anglers would find Tom's methods simplistic in the extreme: he had no time for elaborate techniques, or for any tackle that couldn't be comfortably carried in a trouser pocket alongside his tobacco. He didn't use a geared, fixed-spool reel, as almost all coarse fishermen did by then, but preferred an old-fashioned centre-pin, looping line into his lap in neat coils before executing an underarm cast that was little more than a quiet extending of his rod-tip. He fished pretty light, by the standards of the day – a little quill float balanced with a couple of Number 6 split-shot – but present-day anglers might have looked askance at his hook sizes. As far as I can remember he used a Size 12 for everything, and if that meant he lost a few fish, well, he could live with that. Bait was usually bread or worms, unless anything better came along. One week he smoked out a wasp's nest, and the fish went mad for the pale, succulent larvae. Ground-bait, when he bothered with it, was a random mash of parboiled potatoes, stale bread and stewed wheat, poured from a tin bucket. He was the antithesis of today's roving, 'scientific' angler and wholly un-interested in any notion of fishing for results. As far as he was concerned, you found somewhere peaceful, set up a rod, tipped your hat over your eyes and lit up. Sooner or later, this season or next, the fish would come.

A lot of our fishing was for roach, which Tom loved. Small roach are found everywhere in Britain and are usually fairly easy to catch, but big roach are wily and are therefore held in very high regard. Size, of course, is relative. Roach are small fish com-pared to bream, chub, or carp. A roach of a pound and a half is a big one, and a roach exceeding the two-pound mark a real specimen. But for all its modest size, the roach has a dedicated following. No other species is as subtle and enigmatic, no other species makes greater demands on the angler's patience and water-craft. They can drive you crazy, either refusing point-blank to so much as look at your perfectly presented bait, or mouthing at it with tiny, exploratory pouts that set the float fluttering for minutes on end but never quite resolve themselves into a committed take. Just occasionally you can look over a river bridge and see a shoal of roach, their pewter backs waving demurely in the current, and you realize that for all their easy visibility they're in the one place where they can't be cast to – just downstream of a deep-trailing willow branch or lethal underwater snag. Even roach that are rarely fished for seem to possess this instinctive education as to the angler and his ways, and it's the challenge of outwitting that instinct that drives the dedicated roach angler to spend a lifetime in their pursuit.

There's nothing new about any of this: Izaak Walton, who wrote *The Compleat Angler* and was born in Shakespeare's day, was keenly sensitive to the allure of 'the great Roaches about London', although he had no time for 'bastard small Roach'. Walton fished for roach with a variety of baits, including maggots (his instructions for procuring them begin with the words 'Get a dead cat…'). But he also hints darkly at the existence of a certain alchemical 'oil', that would magically compel roach and other 'float-fish' to bite. '[T]here is a mysterious knack,' he writes, 'which though it be much easier than the philosopher's stone, yet is not attainable by common capacities, or else lies locked up in the brain or breast of some chemical man, that, like the Rosicrucians, will not reveal it.'

Tom didn't let me at the roach straight away. Instead he started me out in places where he knew there were shoals of small perch, which hurled themselves at my brandling worms without caution or discrimination. Only when I'd returned a couple of dozen of these, and shown that I had some semblance of control over my tackle, did he direct me to the quieter, deeper swims where roach were to be found. The first of these was on a steep bank below a spreading elm. The fish, Tom indicated, were to be found in the dappled shadows beneath the branches. The best bait was bread-flake, and you had to drop it just so, at a depth of about four feet. Izaak Walton's book ends with the words 'STUDY TO BE QUIET', and Tom impressed the same message on me. Gradually I learnt to carry myself lightly, to move without sending out a threatening sonar vibration, to lay my line and tackle softly across the water rather than lobbing it in like a depth-charge or swinging it straight into the waiting branches. And eventually I started to catch roach. Tiny ones at first, the 'bastards' of which Walton was so dismissive, but soon a few larger fish of nine or ten inches, which to me were colossi.

I was captivated. The silvery, elusive roach were as feminine in character as the gladiatorial, bronze-armoured perch were masculine. I've fished for roach a number of times over the years and been driven crazy by them almost as often. To catch a prime specimen, though, and to linger for a moment on its exquisite fashioning – on the amber eye, the white gold of the gill covers, the vermilion fins, the iridescent violet scales – is to forget the hours of frustration. They are the most beautiful of freshwater fish and possessed of a strength that belies their Marie-Antoinette-like delicacy.

I spent day after day by that lake, as the sun poured down on its motionless olive surface while the swallows swooped and snapped at the hatching insects, gradually adjusting to its unhurried rhythms. There was an old dam wall at one end, just a few yards across, from which you could command the deepest water. Tom agreed in his non-committal way that it was as good a place as any and I began spending hours at a time there.

This, in itself, was an education. Stay still enough for long enough at the waterside and things start to happen. Jewelled blue and green damselflies settle on your arm. Water rats creep from the rushes and steal your bait. Grass snakes zigzag through the surface film of the water. And all the while you wait, with the rod balanced on your knee, the palm of your hand resting on the warm cork, the line looped over your index finger.

You wait, and you wait some more. To watch a quill float on still water is to enter a state in which time slows to a halt, and serenity and expectancy are one. The place and the moment enclose you, narrowing your focus and concentrating your senses to the point where the frailest tremor of the float is a distinct and legible event, descriptive of what is happening below. If you can't read that surface calligraphy, you will never catch good fish. And it's always subtly different. On that lake, the take of a big roach had a sharply inscribed formality. A staccato shudder, a pause and a steady drawing away. You struck the instant the movement became confident, rather than tentative.

Late one afternoon I decided to try a new place. At one end of the dam wall there was a rickety stile leading into a wood and an overgrown path following the lake's edge. At intervals, spreading trees overhung the water, creating small, enclosed pools. Selecting one of these, I arranged myself on a fat tree root. I had no idea what the pool might hold, so chose a big lob-worm from my tin, suspended it four feet beneath a little black-and-white cork float and swung it out beneath the branches.

Time passed, with the float motionless on the water. Somewhere above me, wood pigeons came in to roost and started their low cooing. Others answered them, while out on the lake the swoop and dip of the swallows took on a last urgency.

The light was going, making the water no longer translucent olive but inky black. My float was virtually invisible now, so that I wished I'd chosen a red or orange one. I glanced at my watch. It was well past the time I was supposed to be back at the house for supper, yet something made me stay. I stared at the float, narrowing my eyes to keep the dot of white in focus. A vast and fragrant stillness descended, broken only by the stumbling flight of moths and the tiny whirr of bats' wings in the twilight.

The float disappeared. No tremor, no dancing about; it simply wasn't there any more. I struck and felt a strong, angry resistance.

For the first time, I was connected to a fish that I couldn't just wind in. A big perch, I guessed, given that it had taken a worm. As it kicked and jagged, trying to make for open water, I held it tight on the reel and hoped against hope that my knots were sound.

Everything held, and eventually the fish allowed itself to be drawn to the side. Carefully stretching my fingers across its broad grey back, my heart pounding, I lifted it from the water. It was a roach, but a much deeper and heavier one than I'd ever seen – well over a pound – with burnished silver-phosphor flanks and a great sail of a dorsal fin. I unhooked it, fixed it in my memory and gently replaced it in the water by the tree roots. It hung there for a moment and then, with a single kick of its tail, disappeared. I gazed after it for a moment, half regretful, as I wiped my hands on the grass. There went the living proof that I could catch not just a fish, but a big fish. At the same time I knew, deep down, that nobody else much cared. The only person I had to convince was myself.

When we'd been there for about a fortnight, Tom took me to the second lake. This was some distance away – perhaps twenty-five minutes' walk from the house – but held, Tom promised, 'some big old perch'. Even better, it was hardly ever fished. So at nine o'clock one morning, beneath a sky of cloudless blue, we set off on the path between the cornfields. I was carrying my rod, which I now kept permanently set up, and our footsteps were accompanied by the soft plink of split-shot against fibreglass. The path, which was bordered by wild flowers – buttercups, ragged robin, tiny purple-blue harebells – led between the fields, alongside hedgerows and around small, tightly packed coppices. In the shadows beneath these, the grass was still damp with the remains of the dew.

We walked on. I was wearing what I always wore to fish that summer: a straw hat, an Aertex shirt and a pair of faded, brick-coloured shorts. Tom was smoking and smiling his oblique smile. Ahead of us was a fold in the contours and a small, dense wood of perhaps an acre. Despite the brightness of the day the trees admitted little light; only when you got up close could you see the dark gleam of water through the foliage. The second lake was, quite literally, in the middle of nowhere and, unlike the larger watercourse, with its serene expanse of sun-warmed surface, seemed enclosed in secrecy and foreboding.

A small gate led into heavy shadow. There had once been a path, but this was now knee-high with dead nettles and criss-crossed with fallen branches. I followed Tom, batting away the rising clouds of insects and threading my rod through the overhanging alder and hazel boughs. Suddenly a small clearing opened out, where the thick smell of hogweed was cut through with the sharper tang of water and decay. We were halfway along the north bank, with the lake black and sullen before us. It looked deep. To my right a tree had subsided into the water. Its half-rotted trunk had vanished into the depths and its branches spiked through the surface. The bank was a roiling mass of tree roots, seething with small flies. The whole place had about it the near-gothic air of neglect that makes the fisherman's heart race.

To Tom's instructions, I set my quill at about five feet, hooked on a little brandling and cast out, keeping well clear of the sunken tree. Within minutes the float was dancing, and I tightened into a good fish. It raced straight for the tree and within seconds the jolting of the fish had been replaced by a dead resistance. I was snagged up. When I tried to reel in, my line parted and the quill flew back in my face.

'You might want to stop the next one doin' that,' Tom observed, as I tied on a new hook and nipped on a couple of new split-shot.

I baited up and cast again. Ten minutes later the quill once again started its dance. The fish did exactly as the first had, but this time I held him hard on a short line, using side-strain to brake his run for the sunken tree. The rod kicked in my hands, but that first breakneck dash was the only shot he had in his locker. Soon I was unhooking my best perch to date – a beautiful, dark-barred half-pounder. Seeing that I had got the message about the snags, Tom finished his roll-up, doused it in the mud and, with a conspiratorial wink, left me to it.

I had a thrilling few hours' fishing. The perch were, as Tom had promised, bigger than in the other lake, and the solemn hush of the place gave it a mystical air, as if I had stumbled into the pages of Malory's *Morte d'Arthur*. I had returned half a dozen good fish, keeping one for supper – a muscular, deep-shouldered fighter of about ten inches – when the bites dropped off, as they often do in the middle of the day.

After watching my quill for the best part of an hour without result, I wondered whether I should start to make my way back. I had left my watch at the house and the cathedral-like darkness of the wood made it impossible to guess at the time. Had I been there for two hours, or four, or even five? The heavy silence bore down on me, broken only by the whine of mosquitoes and the nervy flutter of damselfly wings. I sat tight. Somehow I had been gripped by the certainty that, somewhere out in that acre of dark water, a much bigger fish was waiting for me.

Reeling in, I decided to switch baits, squeezed a pinch of bread paste on to my hook and swung it towards the centre of the lake. The quill started twitching almost immediately, as small fish mouthed at the bait and then darted away at an acute angle. I struck and soon a small roach was tumbling through the water towards me. At that point things stopped making sense. A huge mottled shape, which I had taken to be part of the underwater topography – some amalgam of tree root, leaf mould and decay – seemed to shift. It detached itself from the shadows and then, with lethal momentum, jolted through midwater to seize my fish. The rod hooped, almost wrenching from my hands, and for a brief instant I saw a tiger-striped flank and a great churning tail. Then, for the second time that day, my quill float flew back in my face.

I crouched there, open-mouthed, as the bubbles rose and the lake surface rocked with the disturbance. My hands were shaking, my heart was thumping and my breathing seemed to have come to a dead halt. Gradually, as the ripples died away, I made sense of what I'd seen. I'd read about pike, and seen countless illustrations in books, but nothing had prepared me for the sheer savagery of the living creature. And that was a bloody big pike, well over a yard long and with a tail-span the size of a man's hand. Even allowing for an eleven-year-old's impressionability and the passage of more than four decades, it was certainly closer to twenty pounds than ten.

I knew, as I stared after it, trying to shuffle a handful of fractured images into a coherent memory, that the pike had simply acted in response to its own deep imprinting. Its function was eugenic – to cull the sickly and the injured – and the roach's faltering progress had tripped its killing signal. What I'd been given, I realized, was a glimpse of creation's true face: Pitiless, unflinching and utterly exhilarating.

SIX

IF MY PRIVATE DOMAIN WAS FISHING, MY FATHER'S WAS THE war. For me, as a child, this was both *Iliad* and *Odyssey* in its epic, mysterious character. Although it had been played out just a decade before my birth, it seemed to be located in another, unreachably distant, era. A kind of temporal refraction had occurred, transforming those half-dozen years into myth and history.

Like many of those who fought, my father was happy to talk about the lighter-hearted aspects – the deafening excitement of hearing Carroll Gibbons and the Savoy Orpheans playing in an East Anglian aircraft hangar; the muddy joy of racing an army-issue motorcycle across Salisbury Plain, the precise technique for making cheese in a Cromwell tank (you strained the whey through a khaki sock); or the questionable pleasure of censoring other ranks' letters, like the one that opened with the words: 'Dearest Maeve, I want you to know that you and Queenie are the best two fucks in Watford' – but he grew vague when questioned about the experience of battle. As an officer in a tank regiment he had been involved in a particularly brutal form of warfare, seeing friends and enemies alike 'brew up' in a roaring inferno of petrol, exploding shells and ricocheting shrapnel. There was no way of talking about it and leaving out the horror. The burns on his hands and face, visible half a century after the event, told their own story.

It wasn't until I was married, with children of my own, that he spoke to me about it in any detail. It was Christmas, shortly before the millennium, and he and I were standing in a queue in a crowded supermarket on the outskirts of Hereford, some ten miles from the house in which he and my mother had lived for the previous couple of decades. With the harsh strip lighting, the loop tape of Yuletide Favourites and the tacky displays of 'seasonal' produce, it was an unprepossessing scene. Expressionless, my father looked about him as we shuffled towards the tinsel-draped tills. He was wearing an ancient British Warm overcoat and a battered trilby.

'Those young Nazis manning the eighty-eights at Eindhoven,' he said thoughtfully and quite loudly. 'They were arrogant, but they were very brave. Half a dozen of them dug in over there...' – he frowned at a neon-swagged crib in one corner, as if calculating fields of fire – 'do this place a world of good. Needs a good cull, wouldn't you say?'

I laughed, and an obese man in a tracksuit turned to stare at us, his fleshy features reddening in outrage.

'I do think I felt more alive during the war than at any time before or since,' my father continued. 'It's a hard thing to explain, but can you imagine what I mean?'

Alongside tens of thousands of others, my father submitted his name for military call-up in 1939. He was eighteen. Knowing that it could be months before he heard anything, he went up to Cambridge, where he had been offered a place to read History. The retreat from Dunkirk took place as he was doing his first-year exams in 1940. Returning home for the summer holidays, he witnessed the aerial dogfights that took place, day after day, over the South Coast. One of the most intense was in August, when more than twenty Stuka dive-bombers and fighters attacked Ford aerodrome and the RAF station at Tangmere. With the family home exactly halfway between the two, he watched as the Spit-fires and Hurricanes of 602 Squadron duelled with the raiding party. One young pilot, Billy Fiske, scrambling from Tangmere, shot down a Stuka before he'd even had time to raise his own landing gear. The son of a leading American banking family, Fiske was the first US citizen to join the RAF, and that August after-noon was the last of his life. His shot-up Hurricane crashed and burnt on landing, and he died of shock in Chichester Hospital. Today, his headstone stands outside Boxgrove Church, distin-guished by a small Stars and Stripes flag.

At the end of that memorably fine summer, as September shaded into October, my father was summoned to Hounslow Barracks for basic training. There – under the eye of an authority figure known as The Trained Soldier, a forty-year-old private who in nineteen years of service had never known promotion – he entered a world of Blanco, brass polishing and drill beneath the drab Middlesex skies. His colleagues, a varied lot, included an ex-regular sergeant who infuriated everyone with his unvarying dawn cry of 'Get up! Get up, and meet the sun halfway!' Another, a near-psychotic individual named Private Moss, throughout the day kept up a constant stream of drill commands and admonishment directed solely at himself. 'Private Moss...*shun*!' he would bark, en route to the Naafi or the showers. 'As you were. Smarter than that. Private Moss will advance in single column. Quick *march*!' On runs around Hounslow Heath, he would vary this routine with a stream of erotic reminiscence. 'I told her, I did, I said not bloody likely, you're not getting away with it this time, not *fucking likely*...'

In the New Year of 1941 my father took the train from King's Cross to Edinburgh to attend an armoured OCTU (Officer Cadet Training Unit) at Lanark. Through a prep-school acquaintance, he had been given an introduction to the commanding officer of the 15th/19th King's Own Hussars, a small cavalry regiment whose history dated back to the Napoleonic Wars. The CO had interviewed my father and agreed to his attending the OCTU as a potential officer of the regiment. The overnight journey to Lanark was a rough one. The train was jam-packed, as all trains then were, with troops and sailors on the move. Dog-tired for the most part, they smoked, swapped rumours and tried to sleep. Finding a free corner in the corridor, my father settled himself against his kit bag amongst a party of drunken Glaswegians.

At the OCTU, the cadets were as varied as they had been at Hounslow. Not all were immediately likeable. Amongst the less popular was 'Shitty' Williams, who had spent most of his professional life in Shanghai and whose boast it was that he'd never had to take a white woman by force. The training at Lanark was unremitting; out of a cadre of thirty, only nine were accepted as armoured regiment officers. My father was one of these. Shortly afterwards he received a telegram telling him that he had been accepted by the 15th/19th and should fit himself out appropriately. The uniforms, which were made to measure by a tailor in Conduit Street, were splendid in the extreme. The bill, which was monumental, was met by my grandparents.

Our family has never been aristocratic. To examine our family tree is to see a parade of naval officers, clergymen and other professional figures – all dutiful, mostly God-fearing, some a little dull – vanishing into the mists of time. In the 1830s, in the reign of William IV, George Jennings was awarded the coat of arms that, in worn and barely legible form, still decorates our better cutlery. But for all their undoubted virtues, none of my antecedents made any money. Instead, they rattled along in a state of bookish penury, each generation beggaring itself to pay for the education of the next. At Ampleforth, my father's Catholic public school, his happiness at his parents' rare visits was diluted by shame at their ancient, rust-streaked car. He told me this with considerable feeling, although when I myself was at Ampleforth he and my mother would drive up from Sussex in the Bedford van, which was now in such an advanced state of decay that I prayed no major parts would drop off within the school grounds. At the same time part of me understood that the rackety old van, with its not quite matching layers of battleship-grey paint, was a symbol of their ambivalent attitude to such institutions. It was a statement that while learning was worth any sacrifice, an attachment to status symbols, like the gleaming Jaguars docked in the quadrangle, was to be held in contempt.

Today, if I look out of my North London window, I can see our 1999 Audi, bought second-hand for cash at the roadside. Whilst it was a good enough deal at the time, three years later it shows signs of its share of dents and scrapes, its silver paint has dulled and some vandalistic hand has ripped the trim from the passenger-side flank. It's a scrapheap, basically, yet something in me – some austere streak born of the windy vicarages and dusty cantonments in which my forebears measured out their lives – can accept that.

When I think about my father I remember his frugality, particularly in his later years. The leather-patched elbows of his jacket, the parchment-shaded lamp by whose yellow glow he read and reread the French poets he loved – La Fontaine, Rimbaud, de Nerval – the windows rattling behind the frayed damask curtains, the logs counted out in the grate. My parents never installed central heating; it was one of a raft of practices they couldn't quite see the point of and, indeed, found faintly distasteful. Instead, like characters from an eighteenth-century novel, they migrated between islands of warmth and light: the kitchen with its wood-burning cooker, the fireside card table, the lamp-lit armchairs. As the nights drew in and cold took possession of the upstairs bedrooms, guests would be offered ancient, two-bar electric heaters, which, while making little impression on the temperature, threw out an impressive incense of fried dust. Whilst family members took all this in their stride, guests had a harder time of it. My wife-to-be wept with cold the first time I took her there and was not comforted by my telling her that our bed, sur-mounted by carved swans, was made for Napoleon III, exiled to England after losing the Franco-Prussian War, and that I was born in it, my mother stoically gripping a swan's neck in each hand as she pushed.

The bookish Home Counties world in which my father had grown up, while comfortable and in many aspects privileged, was quite different from that of the 15th/19th Hussars. His brother officers, virtually without exception, were aristocrats, men like Lord Rathdonnell of County Carlow in Ireland, and Walter

'Goat' Luttrell, whose family had occupied Dunster Castle in Somerset since the time of the Crusades. Almost all had gone to Eton together, had hunted, shot and fished together, and had danced with one another's sisters at the same parties and balls. They shared a golden aura of wealth and eligibility, as well as the unspoken assumption that they were exempt from society's more tiresome rules. Many had reported for duty with their hunters, spaniels and twelve-bore Purdeys, confident that sporting invitations would be forthcoming from local landowners – as indeed they were. Some of the older officers had served in India and looked back with nostalgia to a pre-war world of polo, pig-sticking and tiger *shikar*.

Initially, my father was conscious of the social distance between himself and these gilded individuals. Overawed and unnerved, he gained a reputation for clumsiness – not a good thing in the tight confines of a tank – and was nicknamed Jumbo. A studio photograph taken at the time shows a slender-featured young man in the 15th/19th Hussars service uniform. His fair hair is brushed back from his face, his Sam Browne belt is buffed to a dark polish, and his smile is a shade self-conscious. Since his schooldays he had been acutely aware of his ears, which he thought stuck out too much, so the nickname was doubly painful. Determined to wrong-foot his tormentors, he applied himself unsparingly to the business of armoured soldiering: battle tactics, gunnery drills, field repairs, signalling and intelligence protocols, getting to know his men. The 15th/19th had suffered severe losses before Dunkirk, and there was a strong feeling that the regiment should 'do well' on the next occasion it was called upon. In consequence, all were driven hard. Living conditions were far from luxurious, officers were billeted with landladies – a vile-tempered dragon in my father's case – and the squadron mess was the upper floor of a pub.

The war ground on. The 15th/19th moved from Northamptonshire to East Anglia, thence to Northumberland and, briefly, to Yorkshire. At intervals new officers arrived. Those of exceptional promise stayed with the regiment, although most were drafted to units in North Africa, where casualty rates remained terrifyingly high. Of those who left, little was heard again. With every week that passed my father expected to be included in one of these drafts, but it never happened. Instead, he was drawn deeper into the life of the regiment, its long days and nights of training interspersed with dinners with the local gentry, or whisky drinking and bridge in the mess.

The better my father got to know them, the more ambivalent became his feelings about his upper-crust brothers-in-arms. He certainly admired them. They were resilient, they were good-humoured and, almost without exception, would show exemplary courage on the battlefield. He was aware, however, that the friendship that they offered was conditional. That it was to be conducted on their terms, in their language and in situations of their choosing. Life's ordinary, inexpensive pleasures – the cinema, lunch at a Lyons Corner House – held little appeal for those who, on the occasion of a weekend's leave in London, automatically stayed at the Berkeley. And this begged certain questions. Were these urbane young men, as their manner suggested, the guardians of something ancient, mysterious and ineffable, or merely of their own privilege? Were they, for all their mesmerizing charm, really capable of seeing the world from any perspective but their own?

The criterion by which the longer-established officers judged newcomers was at once subtle and ruthless. One wealthy young lieutenant had grown up in a castle in Dorset, but as an old Harrovian was the object of a certain distrust. Anxious to win favour, and discovering that my father was not an Etonian either, he approached him in the mess.

'So, Michael, where do your people live?' he demanded loudly, silencing all other conversation.

'West Sussex,' my father replied.

'Then you must know Elizabeth Wyndham!'

This was a loaded question. The adopted daughter of Lord and Lady Leconfield of Petworth House, Elizabeth Wyndham was a great society beauty, and like everyone else my father had had heard the stories. Of how Lady Leconfield had insisted on her adoptive daughter learning to write with her toes in case she should lose an arm. Of how Elizabeth had had the black sheep at

Petworth painted white for a party – surely a symbolic act – and how, when surprised by an air raid, she had run into the lift at the Savoy stark naked except for a Viking helmet. But he had never met her, and said so.

'But if you live in Sussex, you *must* know her!'

'Well, I'm afraid I don't,' my father replied levelly.

'But you must have met her at Petworth, surely?'

'No, I've never been to Petworth.'

'*Really?* But how *extraordinary!*'

The interrogation continued. Finally, confident that he had exposed my father as a person of no social consequence, the old Harrovian looked round in triumph at the other officers. Their expressions gave nothing away, but he had misjudged his audience and within days found himself on a troopship to Libya.

As the months passed, it became clear that the 15th/19th had been held back from the North African campaign as part of a Home Security force – to defend the country in case of invasion. Gradually this role shaded into another, and the priority became the forthcoming invasion of Europe. In 1944, shortly before D-Day, the regiment was called to intervene in a miners' strike. The officers assumed that, given their socialist inclinations, the men would feel a strong solidarity with the striking Yorkshire-men. And, indeed, they might well have done so, had they not discovered how much more the pitmen were earning than they were.

'Go on, Sir.' An NCO grinned at my father, his finger hovering over the trigger of his machine-gun. 'Just give us the word and we'll open up!'

Such alarms and diversions were few. For my father and the other Hussars there was an almost surreal sense of time standing still. In the mess, the niceties continued to be scrupulously observed. The war could be talked about in general terms, and it was perfectly acceptable to say what a bore it all was, but death, the spectre at every feast, was not to be discussed. Given the butcher's bill from the Western Desert, everyone knew the survival rates of tank officers on active service. Instead, life was entered into with high enthusiasm, and if ballrooms were half empty, rations limited and pheasant coverts overgrown, that was no reason not to enjoy oneself.

In 1941, on leave shortly after joining the regiment, my father had taken himself to dance classes in a near-deserted studio in Baker Street. There, to the sound of a wind-up gramophone, two kindly-disposed ladies of a certain age taught him the intricacies of the waltz, quickstep and foxtrot. It was, he told me, one of the best investments he ever made. To be a good dancer was to be invited everywhere. The arrival of the regiment at a new training ground was invariably greeted with a burst of social activity, with the family silver brought out of storage and the young Hussars cutting an impressive dash in their scarlet dress uniforms. On free weekends my father would take a train to London and meet girlfriends for dinner at Hatchetts in Piccadilly, where couples held hands over lamp-lit tables as the air shivered to the strains of 'Perfidia' and 'Bluebirds in the Moonlight'.

Such evenings, edged as they were by the knowledge that time would not stand still for ever, had a bittersweet intensity, and when my father spoke of them he did so hesitantly. He never mentioned names, nor did I press him. It was as if he were leading me past a succession of *tableaux vivants*. Some were bright-hued and immediate, peopled by young men and women in attitudes of determined optimism, but others were more ambiguously lit, and the assembled figures turned away at my approach. This was a place to which I had no right of access, and I knew that if I pressed my enquiries too hard the entire scene would fade into darkness. There are things we can never know about those we love.

SEVEN

AFTER MY LESSONS WITH TOM IN SHROPSHIRE, I GRADUALLY
began to catch fish in the waters around our house in Sussex.
Tying my rod to the crossbar of my bicycle, I'd disappear for
hours at a time, searching the local ditches and farmers' ponds.
Like almost all fishermen, I was intensely preoccupied with kit.
Porcupine quill floats tipped with hot orange and pillar-box red,
sliding-top tins of split-shot, folded cellophane wallets of eyed
and spade-end hooks (Mustad, Au-Lion-D'Or), spools of monofilament line (Racine Tortue, Tiger, Luxor Kroic). I found it almost
impossible to pass a tackle shop, a tobacconist, or even Woolworth's, which in those days sold proper fishing kit, without
staring for minutes on end at the shining reels in the glass-fronted
cabinets and making some tiny, nominal purchase.

Most irresistible of all were the lures, designed to deceive
predators like pike and big trout and perch. Glittering polyamide
Devon-minnows, just an inch long, which whirled around a wire

trace bearing a tiny treble-hook. Green and yellow-barred pike plugs, red and blue-spotted Mepps spinners, lethal scarlet-tailed Colorado Spoons. I had no idea where I was going to use these lures, nor did I have the fixed-spool reel I'd have needed to wind them in at the necessary speed. Nonetheless, buying them was a kind of promise to myself. If I owned them, I'd use them.

This armoury of tackle was kept in a series of tins, cigar boxes and gas-mask bags, alongside items salvaged from the river bank. Ancient floats, snap-tackle traces disentangled from overhanging trees, mud-choked swivels and paternoster booms picked out of towpaths, spinners retrieved from underwater snags. New gear was exciting, but nothing could equal the magpie flash of some-one else's lost end-tackle. It was never easy to reach, of course, or it wouldn't have been abandoned in the first place. There was always a lurching, heart-in-mouth scramble along a branch or a shivering, thigh-deep wade into the reeds. When you got there, though, and freed the hook or disentangled the line, what a prize! Whatever its condition, your find was always proper adult tackle; no boy, in those days, would abandon anything that could be rescued.

They had a strange, totemistic power, these trophies. Retriev-ing them was born of the same impulse as fishing itself, and even if they were unusable you had to keep them. So as well as func-tional kit, my boxes were full of more unidentifiable stuff. Spiked sea-leads picked up on the beach at Littlehampton. Jointed wooden pike plugs whose paint had flaked and whose hooks had rusted away. Fetish-like scraps of feather and frayed wire trace. Enigmatic scallops of machine-pressed metal. I had learnt one of Tom's more important lessons, though, which was to travel light. The gas-mask bag comfortably accommodated my basic kit – reel, bait-box, tackle tin – and as I swung on to the road, the bike gathering speed and the bag bumping against my side, it was with the knowledge that I could set up in minutes, with the real chance of a catch.

With every departure, there was the same heady anticipation and this, for the real angler, doesn't fade with time. A certain realism creeps in, a requirement that success is a reasonable hope rather than a fantastical, edge-of-the-envelope hypothesis. Yet half a century after his first cast, the fisherman's fingers still tremble as he threads his hook and watches the long shadows hovering in the current beneath the tree roots. This is what brings them out, all those old boys you see from the train window, crouching in the slanting rain beneath their umbrellas when common sense dictates that they should be at home with their feet up, watching England lose to Croatia. It's the chance of a specimen chub or barbel, sure. A fish to tell the blokes about, to photograph and post on the club website. But there's something else, something that anglers admit only to each other, and that with difficulty. That in the age-burnished rituals – the securing of the reel in its seating, the steady tick of the ratchet as the line is pulled through the rod-rings, the loop-and-draw-tight of the blood knot, the quiet swing of the cast – there is a kind of time travel. A return, for each, to the dewy spring morning of his life, when anything was possible.

EIGHT

In October 1944, having fought its way through Normandy and Belgium, the British 11th Armoured Division was pushing forward into German-occupied Holland, with the 15th/19th Hussars acting as the Division's reconnaissance regiment. Enemy resistance was fierce. On 17 October a number of the Division's forward units were advancing from Deurne towards the German-occupied town of Venraij, west of the Maas Canal in the province of Limberg. Between Deurne and Venraij lay the village of Ijsselstein, also German-occupied. It was vital that the advance should not become bogged down; Ijsselstein had to be taken. The task fell to 'B' Squadron of the Hussars and two companies of the 1st Battalion of the Hereford Regiment.

By now a captain, following promotion in the field, my father was commanding the leading troop of 'B' Squadron. The social distinctions that had once seemed so immutable had fallen away, and he and his fellow Hussars were now a brotherhood, mutually dependent in the face of ever-present danger. They had witnessed much since boarding the troopship for France that summer: the Normandy orchards choked with rotting apples and corpses, tank battles and lethal 'brew-ups' in the *bocage*, Goyaesque landscapes with human limbs hanging from trees. My father's diary entry for Sunday, 10 September 1944, records one of the grimmer days:

> At Zonhoven, north of Hasselt, 'B' Squadron suddenly found themselves in the thick of a battle with an SS Division. We knocked out several tanks and guns. Basil Pearson was sniped and died in a few minutes. David Agnew's tank was hit and he was concussed. He started crawling towards the enemy until he was rescued by Cpl Lucas, who won the Military Medal. An 88mm took a pot-shot at Bill Rathdonell's tank but missed. Bill tried to fire back but his gun jammed. Meanwhile the colonel was weaving around in his scout-car, directing the battle. Frank Ainslie's tank was stalked by a German who dropped a grenade in through the turret. He and Cpl Walker were killed.

Balancing the horrors were the camaraderie of his fellow officers, the professionalism and cheerful obscenity of the Geordie troopers, and the sense that every day survived was a victory in itself. But like all of them, my father was desperately tired. To quote from the Regimental War Diary: 'No description can do justice to the discomfort and weariness of it all – perpetual drenching rain, frequent halts, feverish consultations with others to find the correct route, hurried reference to the map and, above all, the constant struggle against sleep.' Overnight advances were particularly fraught, with drivers desperately trying to follow the centimetre of red light on the tail of the tank in front of them, and commanders often staying awake only because of their foreheads banging on the turret rim. Beneath the stars the landscapes of war often took on an apocalyptic strangeness, with the Dutch heathland lit by burning gliders and ruined villages silhouetted against the flame-lit skies.

Near Overloon a German Tiger tank was seen, heavily camouflaged, in a pine forest. When it began to advance on 'B' Squadron's position – a terrifying sight, given its unmatched armour and firepower – my father ordered the squadron's Challenger tank to engage. To ensure the clearest possible line of sight, he lay out on the Challenger's engine cover, calling out his fire orders over the intercom. Three direct hits crippled the Tiger, the only one to fall to the regiment in the entire campaign, and the following day my father was promoted to captain.

However, Ijsselstein looked bad. A long, straight road – the Deurnseweg – led to the village through flat, sodden countryside intersected by dykes and canals: typical Dutch 'polder' country. The waterlogged terrain, reportedly seeded with mines, prevented the tanks deploying off the road or attempting a flanking manoeuvre, and there was no cover of any kind. The enemy, meanwhile, were well dug in, with the approaches to the village covered by 75mm and 88mm anti-tank guns. The latter – the notorious Panzerabwehr-Kanone – was capable of penetrating the armour of any Allied tank at ranges of over a kilometre.

Father Paul Neville, the former headmaster of Ampleforth, was once talking to a fellow principal who informed him expansively that his own establishment's purpose was 'to prepare the boys for life'. 'Ah,' said Father Paul quietly. 'Ours is to prepare them for death.'

Looking through his field glasses at the enemy positions while the gunner traversed the tank turret and the loader fed the Besa machine-gun in preparation for the coming battle, my father knew that his and his men's chances of surviving the day were not good. As a Catholic, he believed in the immortality of the soul, but at twenty-three he was in no great hurry to put the matter to the test.

At the appointed time, 'B' Squadron and the 1st Herefords started down the road to Ijsselstein, my father's Cromwell tank in the lead. To begin with, there was just the rumble of the tracks on the metalled surface. Then the enemy's anti-tank batteries, mortars and machine-guns opened up, causing several casualties amongst the Herefords and pinning down the rest behind a road bridge. In an attempt to unblock the attack, 'B' Squadron continued down the road without them. Shortly after crossing the bridge, my father's tank received a crippling hit from a high-explosive shell. Seeing that the attack was stalling, he transferred to a second tank and continued the advance up the road. With him was a four-man crew: Corporal Beigle and Troopers Dinham, Jeffrey and Statham.

A couple of hundred yards later, the interior of the tank filled with smoke as an armour-piercing shell smashed through the engine. Beigle was hit in the foot and my father in the ankle by shrapnel or metal-splash from the turret wall. Thinking that he had run over a mine, he radioed back to HQ, explaining that there were enemy infantry dug in on both sides of the road who were engaging him with machine-gun and anti-tank fire. But as his guns and turret were still in action, he was dealing with them.

For a short time he continued to command the troop, firing at the enemy positions from the stricken tank. As it was clear that the Cromwell was incapable of further movement, my father ordered the driver, Jeffrey, to bale out and take shelter in the ditch. The Cromwell was then hit again and this time it brewed up. Carried on 'a Pentecostal wind', my father was hurled through the air and landed on the road. His overcoat was burning. Jeffrey left the cover of the ditch to beat out the flames. Statham was lying on the other side of the road, motionless, and Beigle had also been thrown clear.

As Dinham was nowhere to be seen, my father climbed back into the smoking tank to search for him. This was not an easy task, given that the severity of his burns meant the skin of his hands was now 'hanging loose like a pair of white gloves'. The gunner was inside, dead. Pulling the first-aid box off the tail of the tank, my father crossed the road under fire to Beigle and Statham, sticking a morphine ampoule into each. Beigle would survive, but Statham died that night. Supported by Jeffrey, my father limped back to make his report, and as he did so a second troop of Hussars swept past. Ijsselstein fell shortly afterwards.

My father's wounds rapidly took their toll. He was taken to a Field Dressing Station at Deurne, given morphine and coated in burn dressing; shortly afterwards, a Catholic chaplain gave him the Last Sacraments. That night, at Eindhoven Hospital, where he shared a ward with five other officers of the Regiment, his scorched windpipe closed up. He began to suffocate and his life was saved by a tracheotomy. In the weeks that followed, at East Grinstead, he was thought to be so close to death that the Last Sacraments were administered for a second time. He rallied, however, and after seven months of skin grafts, and with his ears now flattened to his head – 'an improvement for which I thank Hitler and the German people daily' – my father and six other Hussars stood before King George VI at Buckingham Palace.

'Have you been b-b-b-blown up?' stuttered the King, pinning the Military Cross to his uniform.

'Yes,' said my father, unable for once to summon an eloquent reply.

One cold spring morning in the early 1980s, he and I drove across Wales with a rangy young sheepdog called Keeper. We had bought Keeper as a house dog but it soon became clear that he needed wider horizons, so we were taking him to the farm owned by Simon Frazer, who forty years earlier had led the second troop at Ijsselstein. Simon had made a career with the 15th/19th, retiring with the rank of colonel. Now a grizzled patriarch, partially deaf from a lifetime in the vicinity of exploding shells, he strode the Welsh mountains like an Old Testament prophet.

The farm was bordered by a stony quarter-mile of the Wye. Simon and I fished it down for a couple of hours in the hope of a salmon, but when it became clear that no fish was forthcoming, we sat down on a rock. A hundred yards away, outside the house, my father and Potter, the Frazers' bull terrier and an animal with proven psychopathic tendencies, regarded each other without enthusiasm. Simon and I hadn't exchanged a word in thirty minutes, as is often the way while fishing, but it was one of those moments when both of us knew what the other was thinking.

'What your father did that day was the bravest thing I ever saw,' said Simon. 'It absolutely changed the course of the battle.'

Ijsselstein did not yield easily. Six Hussars and eleven of the Herefords were killed there, or died later of their wounds. Most of those manning the anti-tank guns fought to the end; today they lie amongst almost thirty-two thousand of their countrymen in the German cemetery outside the village. In twenty-first-century Britain, it all seems like a long, long time ago. A battle remembered by a handful of survivors, perhaps – recorded in a few clipped official reports, and in the history of a regiment that officially no longer exists. In 1992, as part of the post-Cold War defence reforms, the 15th/19th and 13th/18th Hussars amalgamated to form the Light Dragoons.

Only the bleached bones of the story remain. The rest – the slicing shards of white-hot shrapnel, the cordite flash as the tank's ammunition racks went up, the flesh-melting heat of igniting fuel – is buried with the men who were there. Men who, for the most part, spoke little of their experiences and made extraordinary valour sound ordinary. However, for me the events of 17 October 1944 have echoed down the years. I was born on the same date nine years later, and throughout my childhood there were reminders everywhere. The uniform buttons and cap badges with the regimental motto *Merebimur* ('We shall be worthy'), which, at intervals, turned up at the back of drawers. The pale-blue Guinea Pig Club ashtray on the sideboard. The rolls of Elastoplast, with their comforting, characteristic smell, with which my mother dressed my father's fingers, day after day, for the fifty years of their marriage.

Although the burns to his face faded over the years, they remained recognizable to the wartime generation.

'Was he in the RAF?' people would murmur.

'Tanks,' I'd answer, and they'd nod.

Curiously, he never looked old – a phenomenon noted by the journalist A. A. Gill when he attended the Guinea Pig Club's sixty-fifth and final reunion supper in 2004. 'Astonishingly,' Gill noted, 'they all look decades younger than their real age, as if in their final furlong God has finally given them back that portion of their youth that was stolen from them by the flames.' My father was not at that reunion, his own final furlong having come to a close a year earlier, but it's true: he never looked old.

Those flames. Perhaps they're why I've spent a lifetime seeking out water.

NINE

By the time I was twelve I had given up on the Arun estuary and the fishless pond. The pond had lived up to its name, and the Arun, in return for much effort and mud-caked bus travel, had yielded only a handful of tiny, stunted roach.

The Weed Pond in Binstead, however, remained a particular focus of my attention, and when I applied Tom's lessons in subterfuge, I found the fish weren't so impossible to catch after all. A stealthy approach, accurate casting and ultra-light tackle would do the trick.

One warm July morning, a couple of days after the summer term ended, I cycled up there, threw a slice of Mother's Pride into the clearing in the weeds and settled down to wait. Within ten minutes the bread was rocking as a host of small fish nudged at it. As soon as they were fully occupied I took a thumbnail of crust, pressed a Size 14 hook through it, nipped a single dust-shot six inches above the bait and flicked it into the centre of the clearing. Slowly, the pale dot of the crust wobbled into invisibility. It had barely settled into the murk when the three-pound breaking-strain line began to twitch. A moment later it drew away and I felt a juddering resistance. The fish tried to make for the weed stems but I held it hard against the bend of the rod, and half a minute later I was drawing a twelve-ounce rudd over my landing net.

Over the years, I've come to love rudd. If the roach is the shy convent girl of the lakes and streams, the rudd is her brassy, high-maintenance cousin. Everything about her is high-spec, from the dazzling green-bronze of her scales (the roach's are a muted silver, like Georgian spoons) to the outrageous hot orange of her fins. Compared to the demure roach, she's the flagrant child of new money, the daughter of a property developer and the girl-friend of a Premier League striker. To my juvenile self, of course, the half-dozen rudd I caught that morning, all of them close to a pound in weight, were just big, beautiful fish, and catching them off my own bat told me... Well, it should have told me that my journey had just begun and that thanks to Tom's patient instruction, I was no longer a total ignoramus. But no, I thought I'd cracked the whole business of bait-fishing. Fish fine and far out, keep low and the fish will come. A simple question of action and consequence. The strands of broken line hanging from the trees around me, some of it ten- or twelve-pound breaking strain, told me that others fishing the pond had failed to grasp the need for a subtle approach. Hence, I presumed, their lack of success.

Just how wide of the mark I was I discovered a week or so later, when I returned to the Weed Pond. I employed exactly the same tactics: a bread slice to distract the small fry and a free-lined pinch of crust sinking the three feet or so to the pond bed for their larger relatives. This time, though, it wasn't so easy. More than an hour passed before I saw a twitch on the line and tightened into a fish that proved to be barely half a pound in weight. Once caught, twice shy. Slipping the rudd back into the shadowed water, I re-baited and cast, and this time the wait was, if anything, longer. I was thinking about packing up for lunch when, with no preparatory twitch, the line suddenly zinged taut. I struck, the end of the rod plunged downwards and for a moment I felt an intractable force. The line parted, snapping like cotton, and I saw the swirl of a broad pewter tail in the surface film. Then there was nothing, just the faint jostling of lily pads. I stared after the fish, my rod trailing, my heart slamming in my chest. A carp.

I had read about carp. Their immensity, their ghostly elusiveness, their elemental strength when hooked. And I had seen the photographs. Richard Walker, Bob Richards or Fred Taylor respectfully cradling some hard-won specimen of twenty pounds or more. The wet-leather head with its small, suspicious eye. The silver-grey mass of the body, every tarnished scale the size of a half-crown. Carp are not beautiful in the way that roach are beautiful, but they are mighty; they have presence. And in those days, decades before the era of the commercially stocked stew ponds that now describe themselves as fisheries, they were almost all wild.

By the mid-1960s only a handful of anglers were catching with any kind of consistency fish whose weight was measured in double figures. Richard Walker had held the record since 1952, with a colossus of forty-four pounds. Certainly it had never occurred to me to go after carp, but somehow, unbelievably, I'd hooked one. In my mind the instant of connection replayed itself again and again. The roiling water, suddenly opaque with mud and silt. The dismissive kick of that great tail. I felt shock and a kind of guilt. I should have guessed that this was just the sort of water – small, obscure, overgrown – that would shelter carp. I should have read the message of those trailing ten-pound lines. I had come unprepared, and that contemptuous smashing up of my tackle was the inevitable response.

I decided to do the job properly. I had a second rod, a beefy eight-footer in pale-green fibreglass that I'd swapped with my friend Paul for a Ronson Comet cigarette lighter. Having bought fifty yards of twelve-pound, breaking-strain Perlon monofilament and a dozen Number 8 hooks, I started experimenting with potatoes. The received wisdom at the time was that the ideal bait for a carp was a parboiled potato the size of a pigeon's egg. You left the core hard, so that you could push the shank of your hook through it, with the outside temptingly crumbly. There was no float, no weight to hold bottom, nothing. Just the free-lined bait.

I fished for two days solid, but without success, and couldn't face a third. 'If you will fish for Carp,' says Izaak Walton, 'you must put on a large measure of patience.' Well, I'd put one on for two unbroken days – to my schoolboy self an eternity. A couple of hours was one thing; I could easily watch a rod and line for that long. But another six or eight? Fishing for just one or two individual fish, and carp at that – the subtlest and most cautious species in fresh water? Perhaps the fish I'd hooked had been so thoroughly spooked that it wouldn't feed again for another week. Perhaps it was the only carp in the pond. I was getting ahead of myself, I decided. Better to stick to the rudd.

One last chance, perhaps. All the best carp, if one was to believe the experts, were caught at night, when they fed with marginally less caution than in the day. I imagined a velvet, bat-squeaking dusk, the faint silhouette of a tent, and my line cutting through the water as a big carp raced for deep water. I rang Paul and put the idea to him. He sounded as keen as I was, and we went to negotiate the matter with our respective parents. We got permission, although subject to stringent provisos. Teatime a couple of days later saw us trudging the half-mile to the pond, as heavily laden as a pair of Carthaginian foot soldiers approaching the Alps. It has often been observed that children had more freedom in those days, as indeed we did, but that isn't to say that parents didn't have their anxieties. Apart from our fishing tackle, we were carrying a canvas tent and poles, a groundsheet, blankets, torches, cooking equipment, provisions for two meals (spam, beans, Mother's Pride), washing bags, Elastoplast, a tin of paraffin gauze dressings, a corked half-bottle of magnesium trisilicate for vomiting and diarrhoea, and a military-issue prismatic compass. To be on the safe side, Paul had also brought an elderly airgun and a set of throwing knives. There were some quite odd people living up near the pond, and the area had a reputation, locally, for black magic.

I insisted on setting up the rods before we did anything else. With the baits out we sat there for half an hour in companionable silence. Paul, a skilled woodworker, had a sideline in fashioning pipes in the school carpentry shop, and this seemed the perfect occasion for a meditative smoke. The pipes were made of drilled-out oak, and our 'tobacco' was a random assortment of garden herbs crumbled up with a Manikin cigarillo purloined from Paul's father. We lit up, the various resins and toxins crackling beneath our Swan Vestas. The mixture took hold within minutes. Stars flashed at the edge of my vision, followed by waves of nausea, stomach cramps and a sensation of intense dread. 'Pretty good, don't you think?' murmured Paul.

With the ground lurching like a choppy sea I put down my pipe at my feet. The sky was suddenly and unaccountably steel-grey. The temperature had fallen. Either hours had passed, or the weather was about to turn nasty, or both. My head singing, my legs unsteady, I negotiated the half-dozen steps to the rods. Our baits, as far as I could tell, were untouched. I wondered whether to reel in and check them.

My musings were interrupted by an earth-shaking thump. Pipe clamped in mouth like Popeye, mallet in hand, Paul was hammering a stout tent peg into the ground. I stared at him. The vibrations spelt the end of any chance of a carp, for the next few hours at least. Nor, it was clear, was the tent going to be of much use to us. A huge expanse of stiff brown canvas with cobwebs and dead spiders in every fold, it was far too big for the tiny area between the trees and the water's edge. The best we could manage was a makeshift arrangement by which the tent was draped over a bush and then secured by its guy ropes to various branches and pegs. We stared at it doubtfully. Lord Baden-Powell wouldn't have approved, but at least we had shelter of a kind. It was suddenly and worryingly cold. 'Let's eat,' I said.

We scouted around for wood. Nothing, except for green, sappy tree branches. Taking a torch, I retreated to the woods, worried that, at any moment, I might be faced with an irate gamekeeper with a shotgun. The local man, according to village rumour, carried cartridges loaded with salt, which he would empty into the buttocks of fleeing poachers. After ten minutes of nervous foraging, I returned to the pond with an armful of wood. Paul was waiting with the matches and a pyramid of screwed-up pages of the *West Sussex Gazette*. The paper crackled merrily enough, but the wood seethed, and wouldn't catch.

'Squirt of lighter fuel?' I suggested.

'What we need,' said Paul, 'is dry wood.'

He stared meaningfully at the deal tentpoles, still roped dustily together. For a long moment, neither of us spoke. The tent belonged to my parents.

'I'll make some more,' he promised. Both of us knew he wouldn't.

The first drops of rain spattered forebodingly against the canvas, and we dragged the kit undercover. The idea of hot spam fritters and beans was suddenly and overpoweringly tempting. I had long since dismissed the idea of catching a carp or, indeed, of doing any meaningful fishing at all. Paul, I knew, could take or leave that part of things. He collected tackle with the same avidity that I did, but that was as far as it went. Fishing, for him, was the means to an end. The reason to go out and have an adventure, not the adventure itself.

By the time we'd finished eating, the rain was falling in earnest, hissing on the embers and the still-hot frying pan. In our makeshift shelter we wrapped ourselves in the blankets and talked. Paul's older sister, who for years had plastered her room with pin-ups of Richard Chamberlain, 'TV's Doctor Kildare', and the Russian ballet dancer Rudolf Nureyev, now had a flesh-and-blood boyfriend: a sports teacher with a whistle permanently strung round his neck and a concupiscent leer. Since he taught at our school, and had allegedly been the cause of one of the assistant matrons leaving in heartbroken floods of tears mid-term, this was a subject of real interest.

There was also the matter of Anne. A girl of extraordinary beauty who went to the church that we attended every Sunday in the holidays, Anne was uncritically worshipped by both of us. Kneeling there in her fawn Shetland sweater, eyelashes lowered in prayer, long fair hair falling to her waist, she drove us mad with adolescent longing. Since there was no prospect of either of us so much as speaking to her, we didn't consider ourselves rivals for her affections – but we could dream, and we did. The web of enchantment that Anne cast was a wide and long-lasting one, and to this day I know men, some of them nearing sixty, whose faces take on a distant look at the mention of her name. Neither Paul nor I, for all our veneration, ever exchanged a word with her. Years later we discovered she'd married a local poet. *Sic transit gloria mundi.*

The night was a wretched one, with muddy rainwater streaming down the bank via our useless groundsheet, yet honour demanded that we huddle in our sodden blankets till dawn. Our baits, needless to say, were untroubled by the attentions of carp or anything else. At first light, shivering, we tramped home.

Like several of the local boys, Paul and I used to help with the harvest at one of the local farms. The pay wasn't much, but the work was pleasant enough: riding out on the back of a trailer to the fields where the bales waited to be collected and slinging them up to the older hands, men with corded brown forearms and a salty turn of phrase. One farm manager was known as Zeb (after Zebedee in the TV show *The Magic Roundabout*, who bounced around on a spring), ''cause the bugger's always turnin' up where 'e ain't fuckin' wanted'.

The farm itself, a patchwork of livestock and arable fields intersected by a rife, or stream valley, was run in a way that today would be regarded as a model of biodiversity. Woods, hedgerows and corners were let be, wildlife habitats respected. This, for the day, was highly enlightened. If it was too wet for baling, we'd spend the mornings 'roguing' – wading through the waist-high corn pulling out wild oats and weeds. As well as being much easier work than baling, roguing was an education in natural history. As you worked your way down the rows you would start hares and rabbits, send corn buntings and linnets darting, and put partridges to whirring flight.

Another source of enlightenment was a saturnine youth named Darren, who worked with us. A few years older than Paul and me, Darren owned a BSA motorcycle and was something of a local Lothario. Well-versed in the dark arts of the seducer, he was happy to share the secrets of his success. The principal weapon in his armoury, he told us, was a fifty-fifty mixture of stout and cider known as a crown and float.

'Feed her a couple of those, bye, keep up the chat, any old bollocks, *and then stare into her eyes without blinking*. When she looks away she's yours. Guaranteed.'

We would store these nuggets away for future use, grateful that Darren thought us worth tutoring, and it was only later we noticed that he advocated the same tactics for hypnotizing pheasants. You started off with raisins soaked in gin, but from then on the technique was identical. Another of his courting techniques was to take girls Dwile Flonking. This 'traditional' pastime – basically beer-throwing, with a strong wet T-shirt subtext – took place in pub car parks on summer afternoons. The rules, often pinned up behind the bar, were straightforward:

'The flonker stands in the middle of a circle of opponents holding a driveller, at the end of which is an ale-soaked dwile. Turning counter-sunwise as the rest go sunwise, he flonks his dwile. A hit wins the flonker a point, but in the event of a swadger, he has to drink the pot.'

Whether Dwile Flonking was, as some claimed, hundreds of years old, or invented in the mid-1960s by canny brewers, is hard to say. Darren didn't care. Almost every week heralded new tales of conquest to take our minds off sore muscles and fingers blistered by baler-twine.

'Where's t'other bugger?' the foreman would demand sourly if Darren missed a day. 'Cunt-'unting again? Worse'n a poacher's dog, that bye.'

Harvest work paid about £13 a week, which made quite a difference to my life, but the money wasn't the only reason I did it. The farm, which was in Binstead, held another pond I was very anxious to fish. No more than fifty feet across, this was hidden in a wood at the end of a rutted track. Whatever the weather, the pond was always sunk in deep and forbidding shadow, and so choked with fallen branches and water plants that it appeared barely fishable. I had seen the signs, though. The fading to invisibility of a water-lily stem as a dark flank passed in front of it. Displacements of water so subtle you wondered whether you'd imagined them. The place was said to be haunted, and overlooking it, just visible amongst the lichened branches, was a statue of the Madonna. Faded and peeling, its plaster eyes sad, this statue watched night and day over the motionless surface of the water. It had been placed there, the harvest workers hinted, because of the things that local people had seen – although no one was prepared to go into detail about what these might be.

Marsh Farm's owner was a grey-haired figure in his sixties named Ernest Wishart, about whom village gossip abounded. One particularly bizarre rumour claimed that he had spied for the Germans during the war, hanging his washing out in such a way as to send signals to the Luftwaffe bombers. There were contradictory whispers that he was a communist, and even darker suggestions concerning his wife. All of this seemed hard to believe. I'd met Mrs Wishart and she seemed like a nice person. When Paul and I queued up for our wage packets on Friday evenings like minor characters in *Far from the Madding Crowd*, Ernest himself appeared gentle and kindly disposed. Encouraged, I took a chance and asked him about the fishing at the Madonna Pond. He smiled for a moment, a little sadly it seemed, and nodded, asking me to put a half-crown into the collection box at the statue's feet for each fish I caught.

I cycled up there on the last morning of the summer holidays. It was a warm day, with lapwings hovering near-motionless over the stubbled fields. Gas-mask bag bumping at my side, rod lashed as usual to the crossbar, I rode from early September sunshine into the sudden silence and deep shadow of the wood. The path was rough and banked with an unbroken sea of nettles amongst which grey tree roots coiled. I pushed the bike the last few hundred yards, looking round me with a trespasser's apprehension. Next to the pond was an old flint-walled manor house that had burnt down before the war. Now it was almost invisible, submerged in dark-green ivy. Dusty plant spores and clouds of midges rose about my face as I pushed through to the pond, the mud squelching beneath my feet as I went.

The only possible fishing place was directly beneath the statue. In front of me, a corridor of black water, perhaps two feet across, led between the lily pads and the fallen branches. Putting up the Milbro rod, I squeezed bread paste around a Number 8 hook, unspooled a dozen yards of line from my centre-pin reel and cast out into the channel in front of me. Slowly, the bait sank through the water halfway across the pond and came to rest. I could just see it, a pale spot against the mud and dead leaves.

When you're fishing, there's often a moment when a sudden sense of loss overlays your anticipation. It's a fleeting thing, barely definable, as if a cloud has moved in front of the sun, or you've caught an unexpected sight of the sea. I felt this now and knew that it was connected to the summer's end and, more obliquely, to the knowledge that I had chosen to spend the last day of the holidays alone, rather than with my family. The moment passed, as such moments do, and the present wrapped itself about me again. As I waited on the bank, my feet hot in my gumboots, I was surrounded by a soft haze of midges. In front of me, water-boatmen darted in the surface film and electric-blue dragonflies made angry passes over the reeds. I felt, once again, that faint, prickling sense of trespass.

I sat beneath the statue, unmoving, my midge bites burning. At intervals, from the roots of the lily pads, a bubble of marsh gas wobbled to the surface. After an hour, a water rat crossed the pond, its nose leaving a brief arrowhead wake. Otherwise, all was still. Part of me watched my line, part of me watched myself watching it. After my other fruitless vigils I had no particular expectation of a result. With school looming – crowded dormitories, jostling lavatory queues, milk line-ups – it was enough just to be here.

And then, after perhaps three hours, something moved on the far side of the pond. A lily pad, with the faintest of tremors, as if something had glided past its stalk. Stillness again, leaving me wondering whether I had imagined it. Five minutes later, another leaf shivered, this time closer, and I tightened my grip on the cork of the rod handle, praying that my line wasn't transmitting the thud of my heartbeat. Nothing for ten minutes. Fifteen. And then, like the slow emergence of a memory, a blue-grey shadow materialized in the black corridor of water. A carp, broad-backed and deep-shouldered, perhaps eight or nine pounds in weight. In the shadowy light its flanks had the purplish bloom of Muscat grapes. Inch by inch it drifted, infinitely wary. I could see the cautious working of the gills, the glimmer of the scales, the liquid ripple of the dorsal fin. Forcing myself to breathe, I allowed my free hand to creep towards the reel, and still the great fish came on. Inches from the bait, it stopped, pectorals fanning suspiciously. It tilted downwards, the blue-black tail waving beneath the surface, and blew at the pellet of bread so that it danced for a moment on the mud. Then, almost casually, it sucked it in.

I struck, palming the reel so that the fish couldn't turn for the lily pads, and encountered a bolt of pure, wild force. The carp's strength was unbelievable – unlike anything I'd ever encountered. The rod bent double in my hands, the tip jagging furiously towards the water as the fish bored downwards, just a dull gleam in the swirling mud now. I had no choice but to hold on tight. If I gave an inch of line, the fish would be away, racing for that forest of lilies and sunken branches. I could hear Tom's voice, steady in my ear: 'If you hook the big feller, take him in open water. Let him get to his snags, and the fight's done.' A flash as the carp rolled. The line was at breaking point now, the Perlon zinging like an overstretched guitar string, and I could feel the kick and bend of the rod butt beneath the cork. The fish rolled again, just below the surface. A hard young common carp, scale-perfect and unmarked. My heart lurched in my chest. Please, I prayed to the sad-eyed Madonna. Just let me land it.

With a bow-wave like a submarine's, the carp furrowed towards me. Desperate to keep contact, I stripped slack line through the rod-rings. A yard out, a long dorsal cut the surface as the fish turned, zigzagging to the left. The line ripped out again. I got a hand to the reel, but the spool was flying and the ratchet screaming. That touch was enough, though. For one last moment the rod-tip plunged forwards after the carp, then the fibreglass sprung straight and the bare hook whistled past my ear.

I stared after the fish, aghast, as it bored into the lily stems and vanished. My legs were shaking so violently that I had to lean back against the tree. My hands, I noticed vaguely, were shaking too, with long white line-burns on the thumbs and index fingers. I stayed there for several minutes, limp and sick with disappointment. Soon, the pond's surface was still and the dragonflies were back on patrol, with only a few fading mud clouds to show the course of battle. The carp was gone, but I could still see its bluish refracted form in my mind's eye, still feel that heart-stopping force in my arms and gut. Four decades later I can remember every detail of that fish, and no catch will ever make up for the loss of it. But that's the way with angling. For every fisherman there's a ghost fish that, along with the memory of the knot that slipped, the line that snapped, or the hook-hold that gave, will haunt his dreams for ever.

Years after I worked at Marsh Farm and fished the Madonna Pond, I discovered the truth about the Wisharts. Ernest Wishart was indeed a communist, and an independently wealthy one, but the story about his spying for the Germans was gossip spread by malicious neighbours. 'Wish', as his friends called him, was a gentleman farmer. He was also the co-founder and proprietor of a socialist publishing house, Lawrence and Wishart, whose magazines circulated work by, amongst others, W. H. Auden, Christopher Isherwood and Cecil Day Lewis. The firm is still going strong in the East End of London and, at the time of writing – possibly hoping to tempt the impulse buyer – is offering a £900 reduction on the fifty-volume collected works of Marx and Engels.

Ernest married Lorna Garman, one of pre-war Bohemia's great femmes fatales. A studio portrait of her taken in 1930, when she was nineteen, shows a creature of almost preternatural glamour. A glossy black bob, delicate heart-shaped features, blood-dark lips and an enigmatic sphinx-like gaze. Her beauty was captivating, and her captives were many. At the end of the 1930s, enriched by her marriage to Ernest but still possessed of a wild and capricious spirit, she became the lover of the poet Laurie Lee. Tormented by desire, desperate to be near her, Lee camped out in a tin caravan in Binstead Woods. 'Oh, the hopeless acid in the mouth, the fear, the madness, the anger,' he wrote, waiting for Lorna to bowl up the rutted path in her Bentley, bringing goose eggs, champagne and sexual oblivion. In 1939 the couple had a daughter together, who was adopted, with near saintly forbearance, by Ernest. Inevitably, Lorna broke Lee's heart, leaving him in 1943 for the twenty-year-old wunderkind painter Lucian Freud.

Ernest appears to have forgiven Lorna her many infidelities, and her son Michael adored her. In his autobiography *High Diver*, Michael remembers how, during the war, she would abandon her family for nights on the tiles in Fitzrovia.

> My mother leans over me. Dressed for dancing in clinging sequins... she resembles a sophisticated mermaid. After Mother's departure, I bury my face into the cool pillow where the scent of *Fleurs de Rocaille* lingers. I listen for the familiar purr of the chocolate brown Bentley, crunching on the gravel driveway. My mother, always alone, is speeding through the darkling hawthorn heading for nightclubs which assume in my half-asleep loneliness vague Xanadus of Kubla Khan.

Michael became an artist – 'as a child there were no quarrels, no terrors, no rages that could not be healed by running into the fields with a paintbox' – and was openly bisexual from an early age, following his initiation by a German prisoner of war who was working at Marsh Farm. As a twelve-year-old schoolboy he frequented the Gargoyle Club in Soho, and he had his first London exhibition at sixteen. Moving to Paris, he shared a room with Lucian Freud and became the lover of Denham Fouts, an opium-addicted exquisite so decadent that even Jean Cocteau disapproved of him. 'He wore nothing but cream-coloured flannel trousers,' Michael wrote of Fouts. 'Along his beautiful shoulders and golden forearms ran snow-white mice with startled pink eyes, which he stroked gently with the backs of his hands.' Soon the infatuated Michael was sharing Fouts's jewelled opium-pipe – quite an evolution for a farmer's son from Binstead.

Art demands time and dedication; Michael's life, in contrast, became a desperate search for sensation. He relied heavily on drugs and alcohol to dull his fragile nerves: a John Deakin photograph from the mid-1950s shows an anxious, lost figure dwarfed by a massive *quattrocento* artwork in an Italian museum. He often turned up drunk to business meetings at galleries. His emotional life was no less chaotic. 'I have conceived a searing passion for Michael Jackson,' he wrote to his friend (and later, obituarist) Simon Blow in 1988. 'How I am to live apart from him is an appalling quandary.'

Michael's paintings, however, are much more than the dilettante flowers of a hedonistic lifestyle. Lyrical, dreamy and obsessive, full of allusions to the writings of Rimbaud and Baude-laire, they led his friend Francis Bacon to compare Michael to Odilon Redon, and the art critic David Sylvester to describe him as 'one of the select band of English painters who are truly painters'.

I never met Michael, as far as I can remember, but I often met his younger brother Luke, who stayed at home to run Marsh Farm. A quiet man, with his father's dry sense of humour, he was something of a mystery to his employees, but he was respected. I encountered Lorna too from time to time; she often went riding in the woods around Binstead, and I remember her allowing me to take home a kitten from one of the farm litters. At the time, of course, I had no idea of her history as muse and lover, nor do I remember noticing any lingering traces of her famous beauty. But then adolescent boys are rarely attuned to the attractions of women in their mid-fifties.

Michael died in 1996, predeceasing Lorna, who lived to see the first few days of the millennium. In 2004, the biographer Cressida Connolly wrote a book entitled *The Rare and the Beau-tiful*. It was a life of the Garman sisters, of whom Lorna was the youngest. They had all lived extraordinary lives. One had married the sculptor Jacob Epstein; one had become the lover of Vita Sackville-West, one ('a willowy lesbian given to wearing an avia-tor's hat') had been possibly the only female lover of T. E. Lawrence; one 'had done nothing but fornicate'. Like Michael's autobiography, the book threw light on existences of which I was only peripherally aware. Connolly was clearly entranced by Lorna, who becomes the object of her most tender prose:

> Lorna set out to create magic. She gathered glow worms from the side of a stream and put them in wine glasses lined with leaves to make natural lanterns which she'd place all along the mantelpiece. She loved spontaneity and surprises. She went riding on her horse at night, through the steep streets of Arundel where people were sleeping, a small tame goat following behind. Years later, when she had grandchildren, she would go alone into the woods and decorate a Christmas tree, complete with candles, before leading the children out to find it glowing mysteriously. In the middle of these same woods was a clearing with a pond, and this she transformed into an enchanted glade, with lanterns and her own carvings draped in beads.

It was Lorna, I discovered, who had carved the Madonna by the pond, and it was in the same wood, all those years ago, that she had conducted her passionate affair with Laurie Lee. The locals were right about one thing. The place was haunted.

TEN

Hᴇʀᴇ's ʜᴏᴡ ʏᴏᴜ ᴍᴀᴋᴇ ᴀ ᴄᴏsʜ ᴏᴜᴛ ᴏꜰ ᴀ ʀᴇɢᴜʟᴀᴛɪᴏɴ ᴘʀᴇᴘ-school handkerchief. Open out the handkerchief (decency dictates that you use a moderately clean one), fold it twice so that you have a smaller square, then lifting the top three corners, carefully roll them down together. Keep rolling until the whole thing turns itself inside out. Pull tight. Take your cosh to the bathroom, inhaling the stern odour of the Lifebuoy soap cakes that have been cut into quarters and placed on each sink, and lightly wet the business end. Stow in the pocket of your dressing gown, with the tail protruding an inch or two, ready for a fast draw.

Now take the garters that have spent the day holding up your socks, or more likely, languishing around your ankles. These are of grey elastic, with white-metal clips. If they're more than a half-term old, the elastic will be flabby and the garter useless as a missile, so you need to see the Assistant Matron for a new pair, which will come on a rectangle of stiff card printed with the words Kinch and Lack (School Outfitters), Worthing. To maximize velocity, you need to slide the sizing clip so that the garter forms a simple loop, with no tail. When you aim, make sure that the elastic doesn't slip off your index finger and twang back into your eye. Apart from being extraordinarily painful, this leaves a characteristic swelling, immediately recognizable by those in authority.

A dormitory raid had certain constants. The nervous knotting of the dressing gown, the tooling-up with cosh and garter, the silent approach through the darkness. When you got to the enemy's redoubt, anything could happen. Ideally, you caught them by surprise. Your torch-man flashed his beam round the room, rousing the sleeping foe, and as they sat up, blinking, a double volley of garters would be unleashed – shades of Agincourt – after which everyone piled in with the cosh.

It could go wrong, especially if word got out and the other dormitory knew you were coming. As you burst in, you would see what you thought were occupied beds. Lured into the room like Varro's legions at Cannae, you'd then be the victim of a double envelopment and you'd realize, too late, that the shapes in the beds were pillows. Either way, in victory or defeat, you fought in silence. Any noise would precipitate discovery and, after breakfast the following morning, a place in the doleful queue for the swish (a long-handled clothes brush that delivered a cracking impact to the lower buttock, later raising a livid purple bruise).

In my penultimate year at prep school, I was in a dormitory at the end of a long corridor. The dormitory was named the Fisher, and our arch-rivals were the Roe and the Campion (names that will be recognizable to those conversant with the roll-call of England's Catholic martyrs). The rivalry was lent a real edge of danger by the fact that a raid on either involved creeping past no less than three staff bedrooms. The furthest away was occupied by Mr Cornwell, the classics teacher. Corny didn't pose any threat. An ageless bachelor who spent his holidays with his mother, he went to bed early with Hesiod or Xenophon, and thereafter, whatever the provocation, his door remained shut.

The corridor's middle room was the domain of Placido and Maria, the Spanish kitchen assistants. Placido, as his name suggested, was a gentle soul, with an avid interest in philately. Every Wednesday, on his afternoon off, he would cycle the five miles to Bognor Regis to visit the postage stamp shop and buy new first-day covers or rare issues from San Marino or the USSR. He had a really fine collection, which he showed the school stamp club from time to time, and could sometimes be seen through the door of his and Maria's room, sitting up in bed wearing striped pyjamas and a tweed cap, lovingly turning the pages of his albums.

Maria was something else. Even to our twelve-year-old selves, it was clear that this sultry-eyed creature was a woman of volcanic passions. Suddenly materializing from the kitchens in a cloud of greasy steam, reeking of cheap perfume and boiled cabbage, she would rake us with a gaze that was in no sense maternal. We would note, wide-eyed, the frosted-coral lipstick, the perspiring expanse of olive cleavage, the torpedo-like breasts straining against the damp nylon blouse. She would pose for a moment, mutely inviting us to stare our fill, and then, with a disdainful clatter of heels, sweep on her way.

That some frightful tension existed between her and Placido was obvious to us all. What the problem might be we had no idea, but one autumn evening it was clear that matters had come to a head. The whole school – eighty boys – was having supper in the dining room, with a teacher at the head of each table. Through the kitchen hatch we could see Placido pacing like a ghost, white-faced and distraught. Maria, meanwhile, was sashaying from table to table, mascara wildly streaked, twin missiles flouncing defiantly, slamming down plates of Welsh rarebit and enamel pots of stewed tea.

Later that evening we learnt from one of the assistant matrons what had happened. Placido, it seemed, had cycled to Bognor for his weekly appointment at the stamp shop and some time later, as we toiled on the sodden football pitches, Maria had been seen stalking the upper floors, muttering witch-like Galician imprecations. Placido had returned from Bognor at about 4 p.m., at which point his wife had led him to the staff room, where the matrons were knitting, chatting and eating caraway cake beside the fire that crackled in readiness for the teachers' tea. It had taken Placido some moments to understand what Maria was saying, at which point there came a terrible cry and a frenzied digging at the coals with poker and tongs. But it was too late. The stamp collection, on which he had lavished so much obsessive devotion, was no more. She had burnt it.

Thereafter, things were different between them. There were no more cycle trips to Bognor; instead Placido took to frequenting the back yard by the boot-blacker's shed, smoking and staring into space. Maria, her rival for her husband's attention eliminated, celebrated by adding further dizzying touches to her appearance. Her hair became a kirby-gripped Medusan riot; her chest, already a significant public hazard, was now ramped skywards. Mesmerizing though all of this was, Maria's mood could never be assumed to be benevolent. On the contrary, she grew increasingly capricious and was certainly not above lodging official complaints if her nights were interrupted by our campaigns. In consequence we tiptoed with extreme caution past the door behind which she and Placido played out their psychodramas.

A much greater potential danger was posed by the third room. Almost adjacent to the dormitory, this was reserved for 'young masters'. A mixed breed, young masters were usually public-school leavers filling what would now be known as their gap year before university. Frowning earnestly in their sports jackets and flannels, liable at a moment's notice to light a pipe or essay some other parodic attitude, they found themselves thrust, often uncomfortably, into the shifting territory between boyhood and manhood. There were the callow and the smooth, the religious and the profane, the aesthetic and the hearty, the conscientious and the bone idle. Some were an instant hit with boys and staff alike, while others – the uncontrollably violent, or those whose sexual proclivities took an unusually frightening form – would suddenly disappear mid-term, to be equally swiftly replaced.

It was important to know whom you were dealing with and so, on the first night of the autumn term, three of us cooked up an excuse to knock on the new master's door. We trooped in to be greeted by a tough-looking figure with unkempt black hair and a cheerful grin. He was lying on his bed in his shirtsleeves, smoking. Around him, on the sheets, lay the constituent parts of a twelve-bore shotgun and a pair of cleaning rods. On top of the chest of drawers was a falconer's leather gauntlet, the fingers dark with dried blood, and a battered fishing-bag in which I could see a jumble of wire traces and pike lures. With the small sash window closed, the air was heavy with gun oil and Balkan tobacco.

'I'm Robert Nairac,' he said, flicking his cigarette into a white school saucer. 'There's not much room, but grab a seat where you can.'

He was eighteen, he told us, and had just left Ampleforth. The following year he was due to read History at Oxford. From the first, he treated us like equals, winning our unconditional loyalty. He had brought a sparrowhawk with him to the school, he mentioned casually. It was downstairs in the boot-blacker's shed, and he planned to fly it at prey in the school grounds. The shotgun was to shoot starlings and pigeons for the hawk if it couldn't find anything to kill.

'Those look clean to you?' he asked me, handing me the shotgun's twin barrels.

I peered through the breach at the shining steel cylinders, and nodded mutely.

'Good,' he said, passing me the stock. 'Hook the barrels on to that, like so. That's it, and snap on the lock. Now open the breach again and pass it to me, so that I can see it's not loaded… Excellent, that's the first lesson over with. Now you'd all better bugger off back to bed.'

We buggered off as requested. The next day the word got around that Nairac was a decent bloke but ran a tight ship. Raiding parties were going to have to be suspended while he was around.

The following evening, with the sparrowhawk on his wrist, he took a small group of us out into the woods and fields surrounding the school. Apart from me there was Paul, a film-editor's son called Chris, and Philippe, a French student. A tight-knit team, we often did things together. The preceding summer term, the four of us had built a camp in a far-flung lime tree, where we had pored over a copy of *Playboy* magazine containing picture spreads of Mamie Van Doren, Kim Novak and Jayne Mansfield, while coughing our way through a stash of Viceroy cigarettes purloined by Chris from the set of *Reflections in a Golden Eye*. The sparrowhawk was a tiercel – a male, small and fierce. As Robert had anticipated, it did not kill, so he shot a starling, which he then dismembered and fed to the bird from his glove. This was a fascinating process in itself, with the hawk staring quizzically at the gory morsels before suddenly and savagely tearing at them, twitching as it swallowed.

'Is bloody cool,' Philippe murmured.

Robert himself was clearly enthralled by the whole business. You didn't tame a hawk, he explained, you simply lived alongside it for as long as it chose to let you. He was a born teacher, although perhaps more at home in the field than the classroom. He taught history and liked to concentrate on its more sensational moments, avoiding the boring background stuff. So while we were all a little hazy about the causes of the Indian Mutiny or the politics underpinning the Crimean War, we were well versed in the moment-by-moment details of the massacre at Cawnpore and had a pretty accurate knowledge of what it was like to have a leg amputated in a Scutari field hospital.

One day the sparrowhawk simply flew away, a loss that Robert bore philosophically. He replaced it with a buzzard, a much larger bird capable of catching and killing a pheasant or young rabbit.

For my friends, the novelty of having a bird of prey on the school grounds quickly palled, but I was hooked. Ever a kit fanatic, I loved the mediaeval-looking 'furniture': the silver-nickel bells, the leather hoods with their feather topknots, the hand-cut jesses and leashes. At a deeper level I was intoxicated by the maniacal temperament of the bird itself and the notion that one was participating in something ancient. The sense that Englishmen dead for hundreds of years had felt the same thrill as a hawk's talons tightened on their gloved fists, known the same leap of the spirit as the bird swung between the trees and hurtled through the undergrowth at its prey.

In truth, this didn't happen very often as the buzzard was, as Robert regretfully admitted, 'a bit on the thick side'. In the old days there was a strict social hierarchy attached to birds of prey and the men who flew them. At the pinnacle were the falcons, especially the peregrines. Falcons climb to a height, hover, then dive on their prey; in the most aristocratically refined form of the sport, peregrine falcons would be loosed at herons. The hawks – goshawks, sparrowhawks and others – pursue their prey at low altitude, often hedge-hopping and crashing through bushes. Hawks were considered much more yeomanlike than falcons, and the buzzard was the humblest of the hawks. Nevertheless, she managed the odd kill, and the odd kill was enough.

Robert had learnt his falconry in Ireland, staying with a friend from Ampleforth. Those visits – flying hawks over the peat bogs on the Atlantic coast north of Galway Bay, catching wild trout and pike in the rivers – had instilled a passionate identification with the country and its people. Robert had immersed himself in Irish culture and memorized all the rebel anthems – songs like 'The Broad Black Brimmer' and 'The Boys of the Old Brigade' – which he soon had us belting out at after-supper sing-songs. Given that the Troubles were not to start until 1969, the irony of British prep-school boys singing IRA songs was not as acute as it might have been; we were Catholics, after all. That said, few student teachers would have stuck their necks out in this way. But Robert was different, and had the charm and the drive to get others to fit in with his view of the world. His tendency to act first and seek permission later earned him the odd bollocking from the senior staff, details of which he was always happy to relay to us, although for the most part his fellow teachers were as taken with him as the boys were. He was certainly very patient with me. Eighteen-year-olds don't usually have much time for twelve-year-olds, yet he allowed me to trail him like a dog on his hawking expeditions, carrying the bag of lures, jesses, cartridges and raw meat. Perhaps he was glad to have an apprentice, someone who saw the point of crouching in the rain for a couple of hours on the off chance of a rabbit or a pheasant.

One December's day he went pike fishing at a lake near the school and got permission to take a couple of us with him. It was a Saturday, very cold, and in the end I was the only one who wanted to go. In preparation, Robert had lent me his tattered copy of *Angling for Pike* by John Bickerdyke, first published in 1888 but still, in the eyes of many, the piker's Bible. The lake was a day-ticket water on an estate named Burton Park and we had the place to ourselves. It was brooding and overcast, with frost in the shadows; the sky and water were a steely grey. To right and to left, fringes of reeds stood in trembling parallel, like massed spears. This was my first outing after pike and I was tense with the expectancy of great fish.

One of the most popular pike lures in the 1960s was a silver metal spinner called a Colorado Spoon. This trailed an enticing hank of scarlet wool and, if drawn in with a dipping, limping retrieve, was a dead ringer for a wounded roach. With a good fixed-spool reel it was a dream to cast, flying far out over the water and giving a vibrant thrum as you wound it back in. The Colorado was manufactured by Allcocks, based in Redditch, near Birmingham. Most of the fishing kit you bought in those days seemed to come from Redditch. An industrial revolution forge town, it was home to the great names of British tackle manufacture: Allcocks, Milward, Partridge, Rudge, Shakespeare and Young's.

Today that industry is little more than a memory. A handful of specialist rod- and reel-makers survive, but if you want to buy a Colorado Spoon you'll have to bid for one at auction. You see them neatly labelled in collectors' drawers, or mounted in displays of 'vintage piscatoriana'. A couple of years ago I saw a little one-inch Colorado framed alongside a couple of old balsa floats in a Thames-side pub and longed to perform a smash-and-grab. It didn't belong there, dry and inert, contributing to some specious rustic theme. I wanted to liberate it: to flutter it through shadowy water and draw some snaggle-toothed old predator from its holt.

Robert had at least half a dozen Colorados in his bag, their hooks and tails lethally entangled with other detritus: Mepps spinners and Toby-lures, fraying snap-tackle and dead-bait mounts, wire traces, hawk swivels, broken jesses, spare spools for his reel, out-of-date river-board permits, crumpled cigarette packets, a pigeon's leg gnawed by the buzzard, a blood-streaked ten-shilling note, and the cheese and Branston pickle sandwiches that Placido had made for our lunch.

I made up the rods: fixed-spool reels – I had an Intrepid, Robert a Mitchell – and attached a twelve-inch, swivel-mounted metal trace to each line. The swivel stopped the line twisting, more or less, and the trace prevented bite-throughs. The pike's jaws are crammed with inward-pointing teeth, which, as well as delivering a savage bite, can chew through monofilament line in an instant.

We began to fish, casting the spinners out and retrieving them at varying speeds so as to explore different depths. If you wind in too fast, the spinner races back ineffectually just under the surface. Pike, especially big pike, can be lazy and unwilling to expend too much effort on a kill; there's always another unwary roach just around the corner. So the trick is to bring the lure in as slowly as you can, searching the deeps where the pike lie in cold weather, animating the lure so that it rises and sinks like a stricken prey-fish. Go too deep, though, and you get snagged. If you're lucky, you drag in a trail of weed, but more often than not your treble-hook attaches to some immovable root or rock on the bottom. At that point there's nothing for it except to curse, grit your teeth and reel in until the line breaks, at which point your spinner is lost. So you have to use your imagination, to build up a picture of the underwater landscape and search it with care.

Robert was a highly capable pike fisherman, especially for his age. He'd caught pike in Ireland and he held the record for the lake at Ampleforth with a fifteen pounder. He'd hooked the fish late on a Saturday afternoon on very light line. Anxious not to miss Benediction and earn himself serious punishment, he had taken every risk in the book to get the fish to the net. Somehow he'd landed it, knocked it on the head, slung it over his back and cycled the mile or so back to the school through the gathering darkness, making it to the Abbey Church just in time. After the established Amplefordian custom, the pike was strung up in the Big Passage, by the main school noticeboard, for all to marvel at.

Like most boys, I had a mistaken tendency to think that the best fish were the furthest out. So I tended to lose interest as my spinner drew closer to the bank. The last few yards, as far as I was concerned, were just the lead-up to the next cast. In fact, Robert told me, this was the moment when you were most likely to get a strike, as lures were often pursued and attacked at the water's edge. I soon learnt the truth of this. Dispirited by my lack of success, I'd let my retrieve become automatic and was just about to lift the Colorado from the water when there was a big, slow swirl behind it. Following the spinner was a barred, watery shape; not that of a pike, but a perch. A bigger perch, by far, than I had ever seen. Three pounds or more – a real specimen. But by then the Colorado was right under the bank. I drew it back and forth, trying to get it to spin enticingly, but the perch was not fooled and faded from sight.

Robert had been followed in too, by a decent-sized pike. The fish were wary, though, and seemed disinclined to take. Early in the afternoon, not long after we had finished the sandwiches, the light began to go. Robert changed the Colorado Spoons for plugs, wooden lures painted like fish and designed to wobble through the water. The faster you wound them, the deeper they dived, and on their day they could be deadly. But this, it seemed, wasn't their day.

The light had almost completely faded when Robert's rod suddenly bent into a juddering arch. Although the pike was not a large one, perhaps three or four pounds, it was a good size for the table. Back at the school, as Maria fussed excitedly about, chest a-tremble, Robert supervised its cooking according to the recipe given by Izaak Walton in *The Compleat Angler*, with thyme, anchovies, garlic and oranges. Sadly we had to leave out the oysters, not having a barrelful to hand as we might have done in the seventeenth century, but the results were still spectacular. 'This dish of meat is too good for any but anglers, or very honest men,' writes Walton, who knew whereof he spoke.

For those of us who were interested, Robert continued his parallel tuition. He was ready to expound on all sorts of subjects, from dressing ('A decent pair of hand-made shoes and a crocodile-skin belt generally send the right message'), to drinking ('Go for the local beer or Napoleon brandy; only a lunatic orders wine in a pub') and cigarettes ('White Russian are fine; Black Russian are strictly for nouveaus'). These were all Ampleforth protocols and at heart he was clearly aware of their absurdity. This gave his advice an ironic, almost subversive edge. He wasn't teaching us how to be gentlemen; rather how to act the part if we needed to.

One evening, mewing the buzzard for the night in the boot-blacker's shed, he asked me what my favourite book was. I answered, truthfully, that it was T. E. Lawrence's *Seven Pillars of Wisdom*. He was silent for a moment and then began to question me about it in exhaustive detail. Having read the book from cover to cover at least eight times, I was able to answer him, sensing, however, that I was being tested about more than Lawrence's travels and campaigns. He was pleased to discover that I had also read Kipling's *Stalky and Co.*, yet horrified that I had never progressed to *Kim*, which he insisted I take out of the school library and start immediately.

Later, people would describe Robert as a romantic. In truth, he was a more complex figure than that word suggests. His older brother had died at the age of nineteen, an event that would shadow Robert's childhood, and the outgoing persona that he presented to the world was balanced by a deep seriousness and introspection. Although barely an adult, he felt himself out of step with the spirit of the times. He was, for a start, unfashionably religious. Ampleforth and the study of history had imposed stirring notions of duty and sacrifice; in the mid-1960s, even as London swung to The Beatles and The Rolling Stones, the Benedictine monks on the windswept North Yorkshire moors adhered to their spiritual policy of preparing the boys for death. Robert's father Maurice was a noted eye surgeon, a devout Catholic and a purist trout fisherman who disdained all methods but the upstream dry fly. Robert was devoted to this quietly spoken paterfamilias. By the time he left Ampleforth, his own Catholicism had assumed an almost mediaeval character, in which country pursuits and spiritual transcendence were lyrically, and occasionally bloodily, entwined.

In his book *Elizabethan and Jacobean Style*, the art historian Timothy Mowl describes how, in 1597, the Catholic recusant knight Sir Thomas Tresham built a lodge for his gamekeeper on his estate at Rushton in Northamptonshire. The three-sided lodge, which survives to this day, replete with enigmatic symbols of the Old Faith, is an emphatically physical emblem of the Holy Trinity and the mystery of the Mass. How, Mowl wonders, are we to empathize with an age in which blood sport and religion were so deeply and strangely enmeshed?

'Man and woman's relationship with animals, the inextricable tangle of love and death, does not resolve itself by reason,' the historian observes, going on to describe how, in the thirteenth century, Sir William le Baud ordained that a buck and a doe should be annually granted to the clergy of St Paul's Cathedral. Three hundred years later, by the time of Elizabeth I, 'these fresh carcases were still being received on the steps of the choir "by the canons of St Paul's attired in their sacred vestments and wearing garlands of flowers on their heads; and the horns of the bucks carried on the top of a spear in procession".' Which God was being served here, Mowl wonders: Pan, Herne the Hunter or Jehovah?

To anyone who has immersed himself in the rituals of traditional field sports and experienced the near-mystical sense of place and history that, on occasion, can accompany them (which isn't to say that most of it isn't just watching and waiting and rain down the back of the neck), such associations will be less surprising. Put simply, the swooping hawk, the belling stag and the rising trout connect you with nature, whose rhythms and laws are unchanging. There is no pity there, and no sentimental narrative, only the knowledge that you are part of a continuum. But for a man who feels himself out of sympathy with his times, that knowledge is everything.

One of Robert's key texts, alongside *Kim* and *Seven Pillars of Wisdom*, was T. H. White's *The Goshawk*. A lyrical account of the training of a hawk, it is also the tale of a man's attempt to release himself from the barb of the present day. Instead of employing conventional schooling techniques, which are demanding enough in themselves, the author chooses to raise his goshawk according to mediaeval precepts, which involve keeping the bird on his fist for days and nights on end, waiting for it to fall asleep on the glove. Only when this battle of wills had been won, the old-time hawkers believed, could you expect the bird to return to you. Whilst acknowledging the near-senselessness of submitting himself to this process, White is bloody-minded enough to see it through and in doing so manages to snatch a handful of transcendent moments.

To Robert, this notion of fulfilment through self-imposed limitation was an article of faith. Long before I had any real understanding of what it meant, he was preaching the gospel of the dry fly. Ampleforth, for which I was destined, was very much a fishing school – fishing meaning fly fishing for trout – and he determined that I should arrive there with at least the beginnings of a presentable technique. This mattered; one friend of mine, who had gone up to Ampleforth a year earlier (admittedly to the tweediest and most aristocratic house), had received an end-of-term housemaster's report noting only that his casting was improving.

At Avisford, my prep school, the traditional occupation of senior boys on summer evenings was tree climbing. Anyone who had reached the age of eleven was allowed to do it and it was supervised by the boys themselves. You could climb anywhere in the sixty acres of the school grounds, but the full rite of passage involved the conquest of five named trees and tradition demanded that these were tackled in order of severity, like Alpine peaks. You started on a mature yew with generously spread branches – the Beginners' – and progressed via a century-old beech, a lofty wellingtonia and a massive and gloomy ilex to the deodar, a terrifying hundred-foot giant. Only the first two were at all easy. The wellingtonia – the Red Ladder, as we called it – had feathery, downward-sloping branches that defied foot-purchase and made every ascent a trial of brute strength, while the ilex was so dense that the ascent of its swaying, liana-like limbs had to be effected in forbidding near-darkness.

And then there was the deodar. Most boys never attempted it, although those who did tended to go up again and again. On summer evenings you'd see them perched like eagles in a nest, impossibly high and distant. One friend of mine had a telescope, which he'd set up on the back lawn, and we'd queue to see the tiny, football-shirted figures swim into hazy focus, guessing at their identities. And of course those who had completed the climb were a caste apart. They talked about it cryptically, almost secretively, and gave the impression that there was some element of the experience that could not be shared with lesser mortals, with the uninitiated.

I was not a natural climber, I lacked the reckless sang-froid that saw some boys racing up the Red Ladder or scurrying like monkeys through the shadowy canopy of the ilex, and I had no great head for heights. Nevertheless, by the summer following my twelfth birthday I had dragged myself up all the other named trees, one way or another, and I felt myself ready to take on the deodar. I wanted to know what was up there. I wanted to join the elect. So I spoke to Jim Sheridan.

For your first climb, the rule was that you were accompanied by someone who had made several ascents and knew the hand- and footholds well. Jim was in the Second XI cricket team with me; as lower-order batsmen we'd spent several afternoons mooching round the pavilion together, waiting for our brief spells in front of the wicket. Lanky and unflappable, Jim was a very good climber and he agreed to guide me. The moment arrived. At seven o'clock on a motionless May evening, with the shadows lengthening and pigeons and starlings winging to their roosts, we made our way to the foot of the deodar.

'Ready?' asked Jim, and I nodded, tea and jam roly-poly rising in my stomach.

The early stages were technically the hardest, as the branches were so vast. Great swag-bellied limbs, six or seven feet in circumference, that one had to haul oneself over or shimmy beneath; at this stage it was balance, rather than grip, that counted. The route, I saw, was marked out ahead of us, the grey-brown crocodile bark smoothed and darkened by the passage of those who, decade after decade, had made the ascent. At what height, I wondered vaguely, would a fall be fatal. Forty feet? Sixty? We moved steadily upwards, hand following hand, foot following plimsolled foot, and I began to enjoy the climb. The sharp pine smell, the sticky resin on our hands and knees, the prickle of the grey-green needles as you pushed through the branches. I looked outwards and my insides lurched. The pigeons were now sailing through the air below us.

'Don't look down,' said Jim, his voice steady.

With the last twenty feet, I felt the tree moving beneath me. The motion grew stronger with every upward step, progressing from a gentle tremor to a full, sickening sway. I held on tight, feet braced in the fork of a branch, and clambered after Jim to our final position: a cockpit of intertwining boughs and green needles known as The Chair, just large enough to support two people.

'So,' said Jim, when we were both in place. 'What d'you think?'

Brightness falling. The evening air breathless with light. Below us, tiny figures like Airfix soldiers grouped around the bowling nets, chasing balsa-wood gliders, scuffling on the lawn, playing tip-and-run. And even a couple of them pointing up at us and a line forming behind the telescope. To the south of the lawn, the white tracery of the glasshouses and the formal geometry of the walled garden. Beyond these, fields and farmland, the silver-threaded flatlands of Barnham and the hazy expanse of the Selsey peninsula, and all of it unrolling to the long grey shimmer of the sea.

It was more than just the thrill of altitude. It was the sense that we had climbed beyond the reach of authority. That what lay before us was a map bearing any number of alternative routes, all of them vanishing into the future. To my twelve-year-old self, swaying amongst the pine needles, it looked like freedom.

ELEVEN

I CLIMBED THE DEODAR WHENEVER I COULD THAT YEAR, but in my final summer I spent more evenings on the lawn beneath it, learning to cast a fly under Robert's exacting tutelage. That term, he had arrived with a goshawk – a proud and savage creature – and his fly-fishing gear. He had a six-foot, split-cane, dry-fly rod, an instrument of extraordinary delicacy and beauty made by Hardy's of Pall Mall. It was a pale straw colour, slender as a rapier, with dark claret whippings and gunmetal ferrules so perfectly engineered that they separated with a soft pop. The reel was drilled aluminium (a Hardy Princess, I think), and the line, almost the most exquisite element of all, was olive silk, plaited and double-tapered.

You don't cast a fly as you would a bait or a spinner. A fly is practically weightless, just a few turns of silk and feather on the tiniest of hooks. So you have to cast the line itself, stripping it off the reel and switching it backwards and forwards until you can place your fly, which is connected to the line by a length of fine nylon (the 'leader'), exactly where you want to. Essentially, it's a trick of co-ordination. Easy when you know how, mind-bendingly frustrating when you don't. Attaching a fly to the leader, Robert would place a handkerchief on the lawn a few yards away and tell me to lay the fly down in the centre of the hand-kerchief. He'd demonstrate a couple of times. A quiet back-flick, so that the line unfurled behind him, and then a tap forward, as if he were knocking in a nail. With this, the line would roll forward, describing an elegant parabola before straightening in the air and falling weightlessly to the grass, with the fly at the precise centre of the handkerchief.

Taking possession of the rod with fearful reverence, I'd have a go myself. The results were immediately farcical. I'd crack the line like a whip, snapping off the fly in the air, or throw out ugly tangles that would have had any trout within a hundred yards racing for cover. Sometimes the hook would catch in the ground behind me, sometimes in my corduroy shorts – anywhere but in the vicinity of the handkerchief. At which point, with wordless patience, Robert would take the rod and demonstrate again. And then I'd have another go, and there would be another hideous bird's nest. Sometimes the line jammed in the reel or slipped backwards through the rings; sometimes knots appeared, as if by magic, in the leader. Until I picked up that little six-foot Hardy, I thought I knew a thing or two about handling a rod and line.

But these sessions stripped me of any such illusion. The indignity of it all was compounded by my so-called friends who would spectate from a safe distance, sniggering at each successive cock-up. The geography master, a former officer in the Black Watch, would pass by at intervals too, watch for a while and then withdraw, slowly shaking his head.

The public nature of the struggle was, I now realize, part of the lesson. Robert wanted to see whether I'd persevere. I did, and after a couple of evenings I became a fixture, no longer amusing or worth watching. It was only then things started to fall into place. I slowed down, began to feel the delicate physics of the operation. How the tapering silk line would draw back the rod-tip with its own momentum. How the split-cane absorbed the energy, requiring only that quiet hammer-tap, that nod forward, to translate it into a beautiful cursive unfurling. Soon I was pulling line off the reel, bringing it under control in the air, and laying it down in a more or less neat line in front of me. Eventually I could hook the handkerchief every time. The day I did it ten times in a row, Robert lent me his copy of J. W. Dunne's *Sunshine and the Dry Fly*, published in 1924. Like many titles in Robert's collection, it was at once antique and subversive. I read it from cover to cover, envying Dunne his seemingly limitless access to the finest trout rivers.

Such waters, occasionally glimpsed as a distant flash of emerald on car journeys through Hampshire and Wiltshire, were notoriously unattainable: the province of the very rich. My mother had a friend from art school who was married to the owner of a chain of retail stores. In middle age this individual had retired to the Test Valley 'to fish', buying a cottage and a stretch of river near Stockbridge, and leaving his wife and son to rough it in Belgravia. He enjoyed near-mythic status in our family, not least because none of us had ever met him. He was always 'on the water' and clearly didn't wish to be joined there.

My first look at such a river had occurred a year earlier when I was eleven and my father was driving me to a cricket match in Hampshire, organized by the parents of a school friend. It was a hot July day, and we must have been somewhere between Alresford and Winchester when the road took a turn downwards. At the bottom of a short incline it disappeared beneath running water. The ford, perhaps twenty feet across, was gravelled and less than a foot deep; a sign suspended from a chain slung between posts read 'Max Speed 10 mph'.

Feeling compelled, I asked my father to stop the car before we crossed, and got out. I remember having to be careful because I was already wearing cricket whites. Above the ford, the morning sun was on the water, beaten gold, too bright to look at for long, but below it the river broadened and deepened into a great translucent pool, its surface slowly roiling over long, swaying tresses of green weed. The water looked heavy, deep enough to drown in but so clear that you could see every shining fleck of gravel. At the tail of the pool, as it swept towards a bend concealed by willows, mounds of ranunculus broke the surface, trailing strands of white flowers.

Instinctively, I began to scan the water and as I did so the weeds parted to reveal a trout of perhaps a pound and a half, dark-spotted and deep-shouldered, butting blunt-nosed against the current. Every few seconds, as it swung to one side or the other, I could see the pale flash as its mouth opened and closed. It was feeding on nymphs, tiny larvae struggling to the surface to hatch as flies. I could see every detail of the fish, every minute adjustment of fin and tail, and some trick of refraction seemed to shorten the distance between us. A couple of paces, it seemed, and I could reach out and lift it from the water.

Until that moment I had thought of angling as a process of making the invisible visible. Of drawing some dazzling, metalled creature from darkness into light, like an impulse from the subconscious. But here, all was light. Here, to my eleven-year-old self, was a new paradox: an object of maximum desire, just feet away, yet utterly unreachable. Between us lay a barrier like the armoured glass of a jeweller's window. That invitation to look but to keep your distance is a common one in the countryside. Vistas are suddenly glimpsed between trees, tempting the imagination for a moment before vanishing from view behind boundary walls. As I stood there by the ford, watching that inviolable trout, my father waited in the Bedford van. At our feet the river swept through the wooded valley, wrapped in its other-dimensional glamour. The sky was cloudless and no other cars passed.

Of the cricket match I remember almost nothing, but I know that the river was the Itchen, the most hallowed of the southern chalk streams. Unlike most rivers, which are directly fed by tributaries and the run-off from hills, these have their origins underground. When rain falls on the Chilterns or on the Marlborough and Lambourn Downs, it seeps with infinite slowness through the porous chalk before emerging from subterranean aquifers as a series of springs. These become the chalk streams – the Test, the Dever, the Kennet, the Bourne, the Hampshire Avon – which wind their way through the water meadows of the southern counties. The filtration process gives them an almost preternatural clarity. The water has a brimming, viscous quality, rolling over the emerald weed beds like vodka fresh from the icebox. Insect-life is abundant, with flies so plentiful that the fish can afford to take their time, eyeing each offering warily before sipping it down. Often they will refuse all but a certain species: a black gnat, perhaps, or a tiny Caenis midge.

The chalk-stream angler, in consequence, must be subtle. Once he has found a feeding trout, his approach must be silent and invisible, and his upstream cast (fish face the current, so must be approached from behind) of pinpoint accuracy. His fly must fall weightlessly to the water, as if it had alighted there naturally, before floating down, inch by inch, towards the waiting fish. If the angler is lucky, he will then see the trout rise in the water and quietly engulf his fly. More often, however, even if the cast is perfect and the fly a perfect match for the hatching insect, the chalk-stream trout will disdain it, some instinct having warned it that all is not right. The difficulty of the task is extreme, but that, of course, is the point.

I knew about this – the rituals, the orthodoxies, the sporting codes – from my reading. Richard Walker was a great fly fisherman, as was Bernard Venables, who described the chalk streams as 'rivers of idealised imagining…so improbably pure, so crystalline, so opulently stocked with great trout'. I knew that those 'great trout' had been guarded and pursued for generations, and that the names of the Hampshire villages through which the chalk streams flowed – Longparish, Whitchurch, Kings Worthy – rang out through angling history. Yet even though we lived less than two hours' drive from those water meadows, they seemed impossibly remote. Dream territory, like Samarkand or the Coromandel Coast. The fishing was locked up, private, far beyond the reach of the average angler. Or so I had always assumed. However, coming face to face with the Itchen, seeing the water sliding past and smelling that unmistakable river-in-summer smell, the whole thing became real and immediate. There is a sense in which a river has no past or future: it is always now. And I knew that if I returned one day, rod in hand, it would be now again.

A year later, these impressions folded into my casting lessons on the back lawn. The varnished cane of the rod reminded me of scoured golden gravel; the olive silk line had the translucence of weed in deep water. About these fine and costly materials, it seemed, was a profound fitness for purpose. The day came when I could feel their harmony, when the cane bowed smoothly into the back-cast before shooting the line through the snake-rings with a faint, silken hiss.

It was time to put matters to the test. One Saturday towards the end of term, Robert and I drove to the River Rother near the village of Stedham. This was not a chalk stream nor anything like one. As far as the locals were concerned it was a coarse fishery, with a good head of chub, roach and dace. There had been reports, though, that a few trout had been seen in the river and for Robert that was enough. It was a dry-fly water.

We arrived after lunch. As Robert settled himself against the trunk of a willow and lit one of his Balkan cigarettes, I put the rod up and oiled the silk line with Mucilin dressing to make it float. It was a warm, close day, without even the suggestion of a breeze. The river was slow and opaque – five yards wide in places, much narrower in others – and the banks densely overgrown with nettles, alder and hazel. There was no evidence of any trout rising, but there were a few midges hatching, so I took a tiny Tups Indispensable from the fly box. Invented by a Devon tobacconist around the time of the Boer War, and incorporating the wool from a ram's testicles, this was a pattern by which Robert swore.

At one of our casting sessions he'd told me how one evening at Longparish, with dusk falling and the midges swirling, he'd taken fish after fish on a tiny Size 18 Tups.

Tying the fly to the leader with a half-blood knot, I painted it with liquid floatant and blew it dry. Then we walked down to the bottom of the beat, keeping well back from the bank, in order to work our way back upstream. Casting a dry fly under 'real' conditions, I quickly discovered, was a far cry from anything I'd so far experienced. The overgrown banks severely limited our access to the water, and the trees and bushes behind us made every back-cast a desperate business. Wading would have made our task easier, but the river was muddy bottomed and much too deep. We had to take advantage of every foot-wide gap in the bankside foliage, often back-casting almost vertically. Soon sweat was running down my back inside the grey school shirt, while my knees were streaked with cuckoo spit and bumpy with nettle stings. Winding round and round in my head, melancholy but insistent, was the Scott McKenzie single 'San Francisco', which was on Radio Caroline almost continuously that month. 'Be sure to wear some flowers in your hair,' ordered McKenzie. He had nothing to say about nettles up your shorts.

My fragile technique evaporated. I tried to summon the easy co-ordination that I'd discovered just days before, but rod and line reverted to their earlier inanimate status, obstinately working against me. Time and time again I found myself following the nylon leader back to the shuddering bough into which the hook was sunk. Often – a new problem, this – the leader wrapped itself round the line backwards, and the fly hooked itself to the rod-rings. Each time, as Robert looked on with patient amusement and the sky grew increasingly sullen overhead, I'd lower the rod butt to the ground, disentangle myself and start again. Soon the leader was so kinked and stretched that it had to be cut off and replaced. This involved tying three lengths of nylon together with water knots – six-pound breaking-strain, four-pound, two-pound – in order to achieve the necessary taper. Easy enough at a table with plenty of elbow room, not so easy kneeling in a hazel thicket. I did everything in the wrong order, biting off the two-foot lengths and then placing them carefully on the ground, at which point they disappeared completely and the entire operation had to start again. And by the time I'd rebuilt the leader, of course, I'd lost the fly. A loose end of nylon would seem to offer a clue; I'd pull it and, sure enough, there was the Tups, embedded in my knee.

Eventually, I got the whole process under control to the point where, two casts out of three, I was actually getting the fly on to the water. Whilst the fish were in no danger, I was at least going through the motions. Moving upstream, we found a rising fish, just a foot or two this side of a clump of yellow flag iris on the far bank. That is to say, we saw it rise once. Creeping into position through the nettles, pollen and midges rising around my face, I checked behind me. Foxgloves, more nettles and a barbed-wire fence, but above that all was clear. I fixed my gaze on the clump of iris and got the line moving in the air.

The cast was, for once, presentable. The tapered leader turned over and the Tups fell like thistledown a foot upstream of where the fish had risen. The moment the little yellow fly touched the water, however, it went into an ugly skid, racing back across the surface towards me. I lifted the line, switched it back and forth a couple of times to dry the fly and recast. Same thing. The problem, I saw, was that the current was faster in the centre of the river than under the far bank. The moment I cast, this faster current seized the line, bellying it downstream and pulling the leader and fly after it.

'It's called "drag",' Robert explained patiently. 'The only way round it is to put a mend in the line.'

I handed him the rod. A couple of false casts and the line was sailing out. Just before it unrolled he gave the rod-tip a reverse flick, sending a semi-circular loop up the line. This section landed in the fast midstream current and by the time it had straightened out the fly had sailed over the fish with every appearance of naturalness. Although it was a neat trick, the fish wasn't interested. My fly furrowing over its head like a miniature speedboat had made sure of that.

As the day grew increasingly close, we worked our way up the bank until we'd almost reached the old stone bridge that marked the limit of the day-ticket water. Robert tried everything he knew and occasionally, when space was really tight, removed the end section of the rod and cast the line with that. Where the bank opened out, I put in a few prospective casts myself, but there were no more rises. If there were any trout there, they were elusive. The sky was now iron-grey, with an intense, luminescent rim.

We moved up a yard or two and Robert froze. Very slowly, he angled the rod-tip. In the shadows beneath the overhanging foliage of the far bank, eight or nine yards upstream, was a spreading circle of ripples, just inches in diameter. As we watched, the fish rose again.

'Probably a good one in that position,' I murmured.

'Oh yeah?' Robert grinned. 'How do you know?'

'Just a feeling,' I said nonchalantly. In fact, I was directly quoting Mr Crabtree. In one of the strips about dry-fly fishing, he and Peter encounter a fish in just such a place. Naturally, Peter hooks it, jammy little bugger that he is, and naturally it's a real walloper.

'Want a go at him?'

I looked around. We were all but enclosed by willow branches, yellow-green against the lowering sky. Immediately downstream an alder trailed far out over the bank. There was no question of any back-cast. 'You do it,' I said.

He nodded and pulled line off the reel, so that it hung in coils from his hand. Then he started to roll it forward, turning more and more of it over in front of him with each forward flick. Roll-casts – performed, as here, when no back-cast is possible – are notoriously difficult; there's a passage in Norman Maclean's *A River Runs Through It* where the narrator, his fishing skills tarnished by years in the city, admits the near-impossibility of the task:

> There, then, is a lot of line in front of the fisherman, but
> it takes about everything he has to get it high in the air and
> out of the water so that the fly and leader settle ahead
> of the line – the arm is a piston, the wrist is a revolver that
> uncocks, and even the body gets behind the punch.
> Important too is the fact that the extra amount of line
> remaining in the water until the last moment gives a semi-solid bottom to the cast. It is a little like a rattlesnake
> striking, with a good piece of his tail on the ground as
> something to strike from. All this is easy for a rattlesnake,
> but has always been hard for me.

I hadn't read Maclean's novella then, but when I did, years later, I remembered that dark-skied day on the Rother. Robert's first cast didn't quite reach the fish, the fly alighting a couple of feet below it. Whilst the impact of the unrolling line wasn't great, it was still enough to put the fish down for a few minutes. We waited amongst the trees, Robert watchful beside me, with the line coiled in his hands and the fly held between his fingers. There was no doubt in my mind: we had found our specimen trout and now he would catch it. When we returned to school, the great fish swinging casually in the landing net, I would bask in the reflected glory of the catch, suggesting, without actually putting it into words, that it had been very much a fifty-fifty effort.

Another rise in the same place. 'There he goes!' I hissed, but Robert, his concentration total, waited until the fish had come up another three or four times before making his move. Then he raised the rod-tip across his body and gave the cane a single, deliberate forward stroke. The line wheeled upstream, unrolling at the top of its arc to flick out the leader, the fly's forward progress arresting in a tiny puff of water vapour. It was, I think, the single most elegant physical action I had ever witnessed. Touching down beneath the bank, the Tups floated on the dark current for a moment. Then the surface dimpled and it disappeared. Robert struck, there was a wink of silver beneath the spreading ripples and seconds later a dace, perhaps five inches long, was tumbling through the water towards us. As I knelt to unhook it, I was torn between amazement and disappointment. Shaking his head as he reeled in the slack, Robert began to laugh, and with that the skies opened and the rain poured down.

TWELVE

Towards the end of that summer term I learnt that I had won a Classics scholarship to Ampleforth. This was more of a relief than anything else: I'd been expected to do well and I hadn't let down either the school or my family. Shortly afterwards, Robert approached me after class. Somehow or other, he told me, he had to get the goshawk back to his parents' house at the end of term. Since the bird was comfortable with me, he wondered whether I would carry her on my wrist while he drove. He had recently spent most of his term's wages on a 1929 Austin Seven – a spectacular and wholly unreliable piece of machinery in British racing green – and getting it from Sussex to Gloucestershire was going to be complicated enough without a screaming, unnerved goshawk to worry about. Once there, we could fly the hawk and catch a few fish, and he could brief me about Ampleforth.

It took me perhaps a quarter of a second to accept. The end of July found us driving triumphantly out of the school gates in the Austin, baggage lashed about us, rods and shotgun crammed in the back, Gos perched imperiously on my wrist. It was a beautiful day and I felt the dizzying sense of release that accompanies the end of a boarding-school term. We stopped for lunch outside a pub, where we drank cider and the hawk tore moodily at a raw steak. Today, people would probably look askance at a friendship between a nineteen-year-old and a thirteen-year-old boy. In fact, there was no ambiguity whatever. Robert saw that I loved the things that he did and understood that my access to them was limited. Fly fishing – the Rother and its ghost trout apart – would never have come my way in Sussex. Ditto falconry. Being generous as well as a natural teacher, he wanted to offer these things to me. A rigorous instructor, he saw that I approached fishing in particular with the same deadly seriousness that he did: with the understanding that there was always the hard, right way that was frustrating, costly in both time and effort, but ultimately transcendent.

In a sense, I was a believer searching for a belief. Until that year the Avisford chaplain had been a French priest, a former Para who had served in Indochina. Yves Colin had a lethal aim with a board-rubber, and a whisper or a snigger in his class would see the offender knocked half senseless. Nor was there any nonsense about the non-existence of Hell; Father Colin could give you its precise co-ordinates. But he was a good and kind man, and when he was killed in a late-night accident on his Vespa scooter we mourned him. What he transmitted to us was the notion of faith as something mysterious and beyond comprehension. Something that you went to the wire for and, if necessary, died for. He said the Mass several times a week in the school chapel, and as we knelt, the French-inflected Latin flowing over us, at once familiar and exotic, our noses were level with the chair-backs in front. For us, the odour of sanctity was a mixture of incense and furniture polish, damp and waxy in the morning cold.

By that summer of 1966 Father Colin was dead, and the Catholicism of my childhood was crumbling before my eyes, the Latin Mass giving way to a series of cringe-makingly inept translations as a thousand years of tradition bowed to the liberal orthodoxies of the Second Vatican Council launched by Pope Paul VI. Modern Catholic churches were uniformly hideous, essentially sports halls with altars, and the accompanying artworks, usually involving sheaves of wheat and staring, simplistic figures, depressing in the extreme. How I envied the Anglicans their flag-draped naves, their smooth-worn inscriptions, their hour-long peals of bells.

Catholicism's greatest failing, it seemed to my thirteen-year-old self, was its silence on the subject of the natural world. The woods, the streams, the shifting drama of the seasons: these were the province of older beliefs. There's that sudden, intense spirit of place you sometimes experience in the English countryside, that hair-raising sense of the numinous. You turn a corner, and some configuration of contour, light and shadow stops you in your tracks. You've never been here before, but you know the place, and it calls out to you, reaches into your deep memory – its message one in which rapture and the ache of loss are inextricably entwined. The Romans acknowledged these phenomena in an almost matter-of-fact sort of way, ascribing them to *genius loci* – the guardian spirit of the place. Many anglers, I'm certain, are also familiar with them; fishing, more than any other activity, takes you to the places where such things happen. For me, they constituted a shifting series of impressions that, if correctly assembled – overlaid, perhaps, like glass slides – would reveal some essential truth. And if I couldn't, for the moment, find an order that made sense, I was determined to continue searching.

The Nairacs' house was almost absurdly beautiful, a manor house in honey-coloured Cotswold stone, hung with climbing roses. Their next-door neighbour, a woman of a certain age, owned a pond; as soon as we'd unpacked and the goshawk was settled, we made our way round there. The pond was seething with small rudd. You could see them, drifting around in shoals of a hundred or more, occasionally taking fright at the approach of a dragonfly or the shadow of a passing bird, shivering the surface in momentary panic. At Robert's instruction, I began to cast a tiny dry fly to these fish. I had my own fly rod by then: a nine-footer in hollow fibre-glass made by Shakespeare. At £18, it was their entry-level instrument. It was a bit on the garish side –

if Robert's Hardy was an Aston Martin, this was a Ford Cortina with go-faster stripes and an airhorn playing 'La Cucaracha' – but it was light enough in the hand and it did the job. The reel and line were constructed on similarly democratic lines.

Every time I cast to the rudd, I got a rise to the fly. Connecting with them was another matter. They were lightning-fast, and a dozen had come and gone before I managed to get one to the side. Within the hour, however, my reactions had speeded up to the point where I was hooking every other fish. I began lengthening my casts, targeting individual rudd, refining my presentation so that the fly landed almost as weightlessly as the real thing. Robert watched critically, occasionally letting slip a few terse words of instruction.

That evening, we took the hawk out in the fields, working quietly through the copses and along the hedgerows. She was hungry after the journey and quietly, characteristically, furious. After perhaps twenty minutes, as we approached a patch of undergrowth, she froze on Robert's wrist, and I could see her grip tightening on the leather gauntlet. He slipped her leash, so that she was held by the jesses alone. As her grip grew manic, Robert raised his arm, to give her the clearest possible field of vision. Then he released her jesses and she launched.

It was a rabbit, its ears flat to its head as it held a jinking course along the hedgerow. Above, the goshawk flicked from wing to wing, checking her course, looking for the killing line. After a few seconds, however, the rabbit vanished into the bracken, and the hawk lifted unhurriedly into an oak, where she arranged herself on a branch. For a full two minutes nothing happened. We stood there, watching the hawk, which seemed to have entered some kind of trance state. The worry was that she'd had too much steak at lunchtime, that she wasn't sharp-set. But she'd only had the bare minimum, just a couple of shreds. She had to be hungry.

And then, without fuss, she lifted her wings, rose from the branch and, with talons set and jesses streaming, seemed to slide down an incline of air. There was a brief, unseen commotion and the silvery sound of her bells. We found her in a nest of bramble, mantling the rabbit with her wings. One talon was clamped around its skull and the other sunk deep into its flank.

As Robert took the hawk back on to the glove, he handed me a short wooden club. I knew what I had to do and lifting the twitching rabbit by the back legs I despatched it with a single whack to the back of the neck. At thirteen I didn't enjoy killing animals, but I didn't hesitate either. The rabbit went into the game bag and we set off again. This time I carried the hawk, awed by her lethal beauty. She saw everything long before we did; there would be a tightening of the talons, an intensifying of the amber gaze, a readying lift and fall of the wings.

Robert's father Maurice had joined us, and the light had almost gone from the sky, when I launched her at the edge of a covert.

A brief, swinging flight and then she was crashing – blundering almost – through the foliage. She emerged a few moments later and glided to the grass with something in one claw. A Little Owl, pinioned with such delicacy across its back that it was completely unharmed. We stared, amazed, as Robert carefully released it from the goshawk's talons, then watched in silence as the terrified creature flew away; the moment felt strangely portentous. The Little Owl, I would later learn, was the symbol of Athene, the Greek goddess of wisdom and war. And, when seen before sunset, of a death foretold.

The following day we fished on the River Coln, at Fairford, on the stretch owned by the Bull Hotel. This was what I'd dreamt of: traditional chalk-stream fishing with the dry fly, in surroundings of such distinction and beauty that I was unnerved. Towards the near bank the river was deep and translucent, rolling with lacquered smoothness over green carpets of weed. On the far bank, shadowed by great trees, it was marbled and dark. We were sharing the half-mile beat with half a dozen other fishermen, serious-looking piscatorial types with well-weathered kit.

Determined not to make more of a fool of myself than necessary, I found myself a place without too much vegetation behind me and a slow, steady run in front. Nothing was rising, but for now all I wanted to do was look like someone who knew what he was doing. Wishing me luck, Robert moved on upstream. On the basis that it was never wholly the wrong fly, I tied on a Tups.

A kingfisher appeared for a moment under the far bank, a vibrant flash of turquoise. Gradually, I got my casting under control. Another fisherman passed me, a moustached type who might have been a retired air commodore.

'Any good?' he asked breezily.

'Not yet. How about you?'

'Touched a couple,' he murmured. 'Seem to be coming short, though. What are you using?'

I told him. What, I wondered, did 'coming short' mean?

'Interesting! You think they're ignoring the Olive Duns, then. Well, you may well be right. Tight lines, old man.'

A few minutes after he had gone, there was a rise, some distance out. I strained my eyes to see the fish, but without success. It was either concealed in the emerald folds of the ranunculus, or so perfectly camouflaged against the light-flecked gravel as to be invisible. Although I cast to where I thought it was, I couldn't get the line out far enough. I tried several times, yet that last yard eluded me.

Then I saw the fish. It was about a pound in weight, hovering on the fin between two long strands of weed. As I watched, it tilted upwards and took an insect from the surface. The ripples moved downstream, spreading as they went. If I can just get a fly over him, I thought, he's mine. I repainted the Tups with floatant, blew it dry and began lengthening line behind the fish, so as not to spook it.

As I cast, I recited the timing in my head. One, *two*. Three, *four*. At the given moment, I knocked in the nail. The line hissed through the rings and the fly alighted, just visible against the current's glare, two feet above the fish. It started its down-drift. Inch by inch it went, high on its hackles, and once again the fish rose in the water. It examined the fly, seemed about to take it, then sank back.

I cursed. What was wrong? A second cast was ignored and then the fish rose again to a natural insect. I changed my fly, attaching a Greenwell's Glory, an imitation of the Olive Dun. This time I was determined to do it right. I watched as he rose a couple more times and then put the fly over him with what I thought was a textbook cast. He took no notice of it, rising to something invisible a foot away.

'Any good?'

It was another fisherman, a foxy-featured man smoking a Dunhill pipe. I knew the make because Robert had recently bought himself one, explaining that the firm's finest and most expensive range – the only possible option, in his book – was identifiable by the white spot inlaid into the pipe-stem. His conversation was full of such absolutes. A certain product was the *ne plus ultra*, identifying the owner as one of the elect.

'Seem to be coming short,' I said. 'How about you?'

He nodded towards his landing net. A freshly caught trout of about two pounds gleamed in the wet mesh. I gazed at it for a moment, sick with envy. 'Word to the wise.' He took the pipe from his mouth and touched the stem conspiratorially to his nose. 'Try a Tups.'

I nodded despondently as he departed with his trophy. For the next half-hour I tried all of the half-dozen patterns in my box, without success. The flies that fell in front of the fish were disdained, whilst the mistimed casts that fell to the water in a tangle of line and leader were politely ignored. Instead, with serene indifference to my by now obvious presence, the trout continued to feed, fastidiously sipping down some tiny subspecies of the *ephemeridae*.

Experience would teach me that every chalk stream has fish like this. Canny, educated trout on which you expend a frenzy of effort, to no avail whatever. Common sense dictates that you should move on, but some idiot part of you refuses to and you just keep casting. In doing so you become like the infatuated bore who pesters a girl with phone calls long after she's refused to go out with him. Chalk-stream fishing, on the days when you can't connect, is one of the most exquisitely frustrating pastimes imaginable. The trout are right there in front of you, so close that you can count their spots. However, if you can't get a fly to them – and that fly the right fly – they might as well be in the next county. I knew that day was special and I tried to fix the experience in my mind. The clarity of the river. The flash of the kingfisher. The dark carpets of ranunculus rolling over and over in the current. But I needed a fish to bring it all into focus, to make me an insider, rather than a slightly embarrassing guest.

I fished until my arm was aching and my shirt damp with sweat. I tried pool after pool, fly after fly, paying particular attention to any spots that had a Mr Crabtree look to them: slack-water eddies, dark runs, deep-scoured bends overhung with foliage. I found trout in some of these places, but they either fled like shadows as soon as I cast or blithely ignored me. At lunch-time, we went into the hotel for a beer and a ploughman's lunch. Robert had caught a trout of just under a pound and a brace of grayling, all of which he had put back. I told him about my morning and he smiled.

'They see a lot of fishermen, and get a lot of flies thrown at them. They're very spooky.'

And so it proved. We fished until sunset, and I didn't get near to catching one.

The next day we took the goshawk out. She was sulky and blundered about like a stroppy teenager, angry that she wasn't getting enough attention. She didn't kill, so Robert shot a pigeon for her. That afternoon, as we sat by a ditch near the house fishing for eels – an altogether coarser business than the trout at Fairford: you lowered a worm on a hook, waited and then held on hard – he told me what I could expect to find at Ampleforth. All the housemasters and many of the teachers were monks, or 'crows'. Most of them were decent enough, and many were exceptional, both personally and intellectually. That said, every conceivable type of eccentricity was represented – his own former housemaster was often to be seen firing a rifle out of his study windows at the rabbits hopping peacefully on the lawn – and one or two were almost certifiable. The ones to avoid, Robert stressed, were the *mens sana in corpore sano* types: men whose supervision of the showers was a shade too intense and whose advocacy of nude bathing in the lakes just too gung-ho.

All boarding-school boys were familiar with this kind of lower-slopes paedophilia and the system would probably have collapsed without the involvement of a certain type of confirmed bachelor. As it was very rare for such men to turn their sentimental yearnings into action, most parents, if they acknowledged the issue at all, regarded abuse as a statistical improbability. You were about as likely to encounter an active sexual predator, so the thinking went, as you were to be attacked by a shark while swimming on Bondi Beach. It did happen, and for the handful of victims it was catastrophic, but that wasn't a reason to avoid the water.

What neither Robert nor I could have known was that even as we were having that conversation, a priest and former ex-Irish Guards officer named Grant-Ferris was taking his place as a form-master at Gilling Castle, Ampleforth's prep school, where Robert had been a pupil. The role – as *The Times* would note four decades later, following Grant-Ferris's imprisonment for indecent assault – gave him responsibility for 'the discipline, hygiene and general health and well-being' of boys aged between eight and ten. Grant-Ferris, who remained in post between 1965 and 1975, would admit in court to twenty offences, including beating boys for his sexual gratification. And yet, at the time of the trial, Leeds Crown Court received 3,500 letters of support for the disgraced priest. A friend of mine who was a pupil at Gilling when Grant-Ferris was a form-teacher there refused point-blank to believe the charges.

When Robert arrived at Ampleforth, monitors, as the prefects were called, were allowed to cane their juniors. Most were decent enough not to exercise this privilege, but a few took it to excess. Robert was one of a number of boys who became the target of a cabal of older sadists, to whose vicious abuse of power the rabbit-sniping housemaster turned a blind, or at least an ineffectual, eye. This had made Robert's early terms very miserable indeed and he had turned to boxing as a means of retaliation. Naturally talented, impelled by fury and distress, he had soon become lethally efficient with his fists and thereafter he had been left alone. When he became head of the school – and he is remembered to this day as one of the most charismatic individuals to have held that position – his first official action was to ban the beating of boys by their peers.

Eel-fishing is a chaotic, almost slapstick business. They lash around, tie themselves in knots and have to be chased through the grass, which is probably why Robert chose that particular time to relive these events. I might easily not have noticed just how pale he had become, or how clipped his words. As others would later observe, there was a deeply fatalistic side to him, which occasionally got the upper hand. In the evenings, after supper, he would pour us each a finger of Napoleon brandy and play Beatles records. He was particularly attached to the slower, sadder songs like 'Norwegian Wood' and 'Nowhere Man', and we'd sit in pensive near-silence, stripping the wet silk lines off the fly reels and laying them to dry in coils over the oak beams.

That evening, Maurice drove us to a private lake near Withington. It lay, promisingly, at the end of a long, winding track: a narrow two-acre rectangle, enclosed by tall trees, which, as the sun fell, became grey silhouettes. It was a still evening and the air was heavy with the smell of the water. At intervals, trout would rise with an unguarded gulping sound, leaving extravagantly spreading ripples. Putting up my rod, I chose a plain black wet fly with soft hen-hackles, something that would look like a drowning insect against the fading light. I had positioned myself at the lower end of one of the long banks; the others were at right angles to me. So solitary was the place, and so quiet, it was hard to imagine that there was anyone else for miles. I began to cast, sending out the longest line I could, letting the fly sink an inch or two beneath the surface film and then, very slowly, twitching it in. Robert, thirty yards away, let me get on with it and I understood that he wanted me to show Maurice what he'd taught me.

A quarter of an hour later I had just cast for perhaps the tenth time and was giving the fly a moment to sink. The silk line snaked out in front of me, cushioned by surface tension, and I was staring at it, half-mesmerized, when the water around my fly soundlessly infolded. For a second or two I didn't realize what I'd seen, and then the leader twitched and the slack line slid away. I lifted the rod, felt a shuddering resistance and saw a deep, dull flash. The fish ran straight for the centre of the lake, tearing the line through my fingers and making the reel-ratchet snarl. I knew enough to hold the rod high and keep a finger on the spool to prevent over-runs, and gradually I turned the fish, winding in the slack so that I could play it straight off the reel. The fish kept deep, boring down hard against the bend of the rod, trying to run for the lake's dark centre. I saw it clearly only when Robert appeared beside me with a landing net.

'Well hooked,' he said quietly, lifting net and trout from the water. 'That's a really good one.'

And it was. Well over the pound, and elegantly marked with dark umber spots, it was pretty much perfect. I hit it on the back of the head; it shivered for a moment and was dead. Nodding his approval, Robert disappeared into the dusk. As I fished on, I glanced down every few minutes to check that the trout was really there, stiffening and silvery in its shroud of wet grass. Twenty minutes later another fish drew my line taut, and when we finally packed up, and made our way through the enfolding darkness to the car, we'd caught a brace each. The lake was probably stocked, and the fish almost certainly lacked the preternatural caution of the wild trout on the Coln, but for me that evening was a rite of passage. Whatever else I might become, for good or ill, I was now a fly fisherman.

THIRTEEN

ON 10 FEBRUARY 1938, WITH THE WORLD POISED ON THE brink of the most destructive war in history, the committee of the Flyfisher's Club called a meeting at their headquarters at 36 Piccadilly, on the corner of Swallow Street. The subsequent debate, attended by the greatest fly fishermen of the day, was probably the most ferocious in the annals of angling. Even a decade later, in the words of H. D. Turing, then editor of the *Salmon and Trout Magazine*, the controversy was still raging, 'rising and waning, like a recurrent thunderstorm'. The issue, and the official title of the debate, was 'Nymph Fishing in Chalk Streams'.

In the early days of the nineteenth century, those who fished on the chalk streams did so with the wet, or sunk, fly. They cast this downstream with the current, preferably on a windy day, when the glassy surface of the water was disturbed and the fish easier to deceive. To the Scottish angling writer W. C. Stewart, however, this approach was counter-productive.

'The great error of fly fishing, as usually practised, and as usually recommended to be practised in books, is that the angler fishes downstream, whereas he should fish up,' he wrote in *The Practical Angler*, published in 1857. Trout face upstream, Stewart explained, 'so that the angler fishing down will be seen by them twenty yards off, whereas the angler fishing up will be unseen, although he be but a few yards in their rear.' He may 'make his flies light softly as a gossamer', but this will count for nothing if the trout has already seen him. Fishing upstream makes hooking easier, disturbs the water less than the downstream method and enables a more natural presentation of the fly. Whilst Stewart's case was irrefutable, it meant that fly fishermen had to master a much subtler art than before. Fishing downstream and across, the angler has the current on his side, and even the poorest cast is quickly ironed out by the stream. Upstream fishing demands pinpoint casting, as well as the skill to remain in contact with a fly that is being carried towards you, often quite fast, without in any way affecting the naturalness of its drift.

When Stewart was making the case for upstream fishing, he was referring to the wet fly. Nevertheless, a few years earlier, a Devon tackle-maker named George Pulman had begun preaching the gospel of the dry fly. In the third edition of *The Vade-Mecum of Fly-Fishing for Trout*, published in 1851, Pulman describes how, when the angler discovers a rising fish, he should dry his fly by flicking it back and forth a few times ('false casting'), and then, with all the precision of which he is capable, place this fly on the water just upstream of the rising fish, so that it floats back over it. By the later years of the nineteenth century, upstream dry-fly fishing had taken hold on the chalk streams. Here, finally, was a method that fully reflected their dreamy slowness, their pellucid clarity.

The high priests of the Victorian dry-fly era were G. S. Marryat and F. M. Halford. Marryat, the older man, was the practitioner par excellence and is often said to have been the greatest fly fisherman who ever lived. Halford was the theorist, applying himself with typically Victorian fixity of purpose to the question of how best to imitate the natural fly on the water. His researches, based on close observation of insect life, gave birth to a series of classic dry-fly patterns, some of which are still in use today. Halford's studies coincided with an explosion in the popularity of fishing. This was brought about, at least in part, by the growth of the railways, which gave metropolitan anglers access to previously inaccessible waters. But the chalk streams, being a limited resource and costly to maintain, were to become the preserve of the few. A culture of exclusivity came into being. There were the fly fishermen, with their split-cane rods and silken lines, and there were the rest. The coarse anglers. The roach angler on the canal towpath, the tench-man by his lake, the pike-hunter in his Thames-side punt.

Halford's era was also the heyday of Empire. The prevailing

notion, fostered by the public schools, was that the well-born Briton should demonstrate the Christian principles of fairness, decency and the straight bat. That his role, whether taking his place in the family pew or dispensing justice in some far-flung jungle clearing, was to follow the rules. And nowhere were these more arcane than on the chalk streams. Halford the pragmatist, a man of empirical bent, made clear that he advocated dry-fly fishing and 'exact imitation' because this was the most effective way to catch trout. The generation of anglers who followed him, however, turned his theories into rigid orthodoxy. For the true gentleman, the dry fly was the only way. Its very difficulty endowed it with a moral character; other methods were simply too easy to be fair.

There were the purists and there were the ultra-purists. The purists allowed themselves the luxury of 'speculative' casting: that is, casting to a trout that wasn't rising, or to a place where experience told them a fish might be lying. The ultra-purists disdained even this. For them, Halford's dictum was an article of faith. The fish must be seen to rise and must be fished for 'with the best possible imitation' of the fly in question. If nothing was moving, you simply sat back and waited. The Piscatorial Society, England's oldest fishing club, still abides by this rule.

To read Victorian and Edwardian angling memoirs is to get a keen sense of this era and its atmosphere. One can imagine the fly fisherman, City-bound during the week, waiting on the platform of a steam-filled Waterloo with his valise and his rod-bags. He will be weekending in some reposeful fold of the Hampshire hills – in Martyr Worthy, perhaps, or Itchen Abbas – and turning his attention from commodity prices and ocean-going cargo to the imitation of delicate, gossamer-winged *ephemeridae* and the deceiving of wary trout. In the place of the bustling crowds, there will be the peace of the river bank. A sense of certainty pervades such scenes. Certainty that this is how things should be, certainty that they will continue thus for ever. The valleys will always be green, the cuckoos will always call in the water meadows, the mayfly will always hatch.

In 1910, however, a stubborn voice obtruded on the idyll. *Minor Tactics of the Chalk Stream* was the work of G. E. M. Skues, a lawyer and lifelong free-thinker who had learnt his fly fishing while at Winchester College. Despite its unassuming title, the book caused a furore. While on the Itchen, Skues wrote, he had had occasion to watch fish that, while not rising, were lying high in the water and switching from side to side as if feeding. They were taking nymphs.

The nymph, a translucent creature with a segmented body, is the second stage in the life of an aquatic fly. Born from the egg, it forages in weeds or on the river bed for several months and then wriggles its way to the surface. Once there, the nymphal husk splits and the adult fly emerges, delicate and iridescent-winged. Calculating that trout spent much more time feeding on nymphs than on fully hatched surface flies, Skues set about imitating these elusive creatures. The result was a series of sparely dressed patterns quite unlike any existing flies. Casting these upstream, so that they had time to sink, he dead-drifted them past the waiting trout. The difficulty lay in knowing when to strike. When fishing the dry fly you can see the rise, but when fishing the nymph it's much harder. Skues taught himself to strike at the slightest check or tautening of the leader, the smallest bulging of the water, or merely a half-glimpsed gleam as the fish swung to the fly.

Skues began to catch trout on his nymphs and, more importantly, to catch them when the fish were not taking flies on the surface. Nymphing, it was clear, could greatly extend the fly-fisherman's day: no longer did he have to wait for the morning or evening rise, which could be short-lived or even non-existent. You might have thought that the chalk-stream fraternity would have been grateful to Skues for thus enlightening them, yet with very few exceptions they condemned him.

To fish the nymph, the purists claimed, contravened sporting ethics. The technique would lead to the uncontrolled use of the sunk fly, which many considered little better than poaching. Although these fears were misplaced, the purists' protest was more a matter of emotion than of logic. They had subscribed to an orthodoxy, seen it challenged and were outraged. 'A trout killed on a nymph in a chalk stream is one lost to the dry fly,' lamented

J. C. Mottram, who wrote for *The Field* magazine under the pseudonym 'Jim-Jam'.

In 1921, Skues responded with a second book, *The Way of a Trout with a Fly*, in which he made his opinion of the Halfordians clear. 'An authority that lays down law and dogmatizes is a narcotic, a soporific, a stupifier, an opiate,' he wrote. As the years passed, however, the voice of the dry-fly purists grew louder and their objections to nymph fishing more strident. A spate of correspondence in the *Journal of the Flyfisher's Club* brought the matter to a head, and the Great Debate was announced.

Despite the fact that Skues was by then eighty years old, his prosecutors gave him no quarter. Sir Joseph Ball, a barrister, led the attack, claiming that Halford himself had 'rejected the nymph'. This was a misrepresentation of Halford's position, but having died almost a quarter of a century earlier, that 'Ipsissimus of the Dry Fly cult', as the historian Charles Chevenix Trench described him, was in no position to set the record straight. 'Jim-Jam' Mottram supported Ball, as did most of the others present. Skues's side was taken by J. W. Hills, the Conservative MP for Ripon. Whilst the two of them could probably have made their case more forcefully, they didn't really need to, because the truth was self-evident: nymph fishing was at least as demanding an art as that of the dry fly, as well as a useful complement to it.

So what was it, exactly, that so concerned the purists? Why, in the month in which the Wehrmacht marched into Austria, were intelligent men concerning themselves with such minutiae? My own theory is that, as so often with the English, the conversation was actually about something else. It was about identity and change; about the way that the foundations of the upper-middle-class world had begun to crumble. The ancient certainties had come to an end with the Great War, and the old virtues of patriotism, piety and deference to authority had been thrown open to question. Five years to the day before the Great Debate, the Oxford Union had carried the motion 'That this House will in no circumstances fight for King and Country'. For two decades the haute bourgeoisie had been fighting a rearguard action in defence of its values; the law of the dry fly according to Halford, austere and unambiguous as it was, had everything in common with those values. In a sense the dispute exposed aspects of the English character that had been at war for a thousand years. Norman adherence to form, tradition and hierarchy; Anglo-Saxon stubbornness and democratic instinct. There was more than a little of Cromwell in Skues and much that was Cavalier in the Halfordian old guard.

Dry-fly fishing is an art, but it is conceptually straightforward. It unfolds in two dimensions; it succeeds or it fails; it is clear, hard-edged and Apollonian. Nymph fishing occurs in three dimensions, and is instinctive, fluid and ambiguous. A similar distinction was drawn in mediaeval falconry, where birds that rose above their prey and fell on them from above were dubbed 'noble', and those that took the quarry in direct chase 'ignoble'. Although subtle differences, to those who defined themselves by where they drew the line, they were profound ones.

I remember going with Robert and his father to a syndicate-run fishery in Gloucestershire. To one side of the main lake was a small translucent pool, lit to its considerable depth by shafts of sunlight. Some twenty feet down, a pair of large trout could be seen circling. As I watched, an angler stalked them with a tiny, unweighted nymph. Given the depth, the refraction of the light and the fact that the nymph could be moved only in extreme slow motion, this was a highly complex task. Maurice, however, had his reservations. To permit nymph fishing was, sooner or later, to open the door to all sorts of questionable behaviour. Personally, he preferred to confine himself to the dry fly. And this was in 1966.

I don't remember Robert so much as mentioning nymph fishing. The book he lent me when I learnt to cast, J. W. Dunne's *Sunshine and the Dry Fly*, was essentially an updating of Halford. A fish sees a floating fly against the light, delicate and transparent, but Halford produced his imitations using opaque materials. From the trout's perspective they would have been black silhouettes. Dunne addressed himself to the issue of translucency and after many experiments discovered that if he painted the shanks of his hooks white, then dressed the bodies of his flies with artificial silk and oiled them, his artificials achieved the gauzy transparency of the naturals as seen from below. Dunne's book was published in 1924 and his theories have now largely been forgotten. Hardy's of Pall Mall, however, continued to tie flies to his specification until well into the 1960s, and Robert swore by their effectiveness.

Even today, a century after the publication of Skues's *Minor Tactics of the Chalk Stream*, there are those who only ever use the dry fly and never the nymph. Whilst I'm not one of them, I can understand that choice and I can feel the pull of that unconditional position. Upstream nymph fishing is a demanding art, and it took me many years and many missed fish even to begin to get the hang of it. But it hasn't the poetry and the airy lightness of the dry fly. It doesn't, for the duration of a stolen afternoon or evening, bring back the age of gold. I may yet vote against Skues in the Great Debate.

FOURTEEN

CATCHING THE AMPLEFORTH TRAIN FROM KING'S CROSS was a ritual of unparalleled grimness. My father would drive me up to London from Sussex and, after a ceremonial lunch at a Polish restaurant whose name and location I never quite established, we would arrive early at the station with my trunk. The minutes passed slowly and our conversation was halting. For older boys it was a last chance of peacockery before the austerity of school. They would drift past us in Regency jackets and high-collared shirts, trailing patchouli-scented chiffon scarves and, in many cases, smoking.

Intimacy was impossible under such unnerving circumstances, and my father and I would part brusquely, both glad to get away. In my first term I found a seat on the train opposite a languid sophisticate of fifteen, who glanced with amusement at my regulation sports coat and black school tie.

'You must be new,' he said, unzipping an overnight bag

and taking out a silver cocktail shaker. When I nodded, he filled the silver top of the shaker and passed it to me. I took a hesitant sip of the delicate, effervescent drink. 'Hock and seltzer,' he explained. 'My father makes it up for me at the beginning of every term.' It was a gesture of such unhesitating decency that I nearly burst into tears there and then.

The journey took four hours, and it seemed to get colder and darker with every mile. Buses were waiting at York Station, ten of them, one for each house. It was a journey of about twenty-five miles and you saw the school in the distance long before you got there. When we'd taken delivery of our trunks we went into house supper and were directed to a table shared with some second-year boys. In front of us were stacks of sliced white bread and bowls of pale-orange soup of indeterminate taste. Our house-master, Father Edward, presided over the revels. While we were eating, a small monkey appeared at the window and sat there looking in at us, its face wrinkled in melancholy. After a minute or so, when I was more or less certain that it wasn't a hallucination, I hesitantly mentioned its presence.

'Yes, that's the house monkey,' a second-year explained. 'If someone does something really appalling and no one owns up, the monkey is beaten.'

I met the creature's sad gaze. 'Of course,' I said.

The following day, the new boys were assembled, to be addressed by the head boy, a figure of some eminence named Gus

Whitehead. He spoke to us, with inspiring fervour, of the school spirit (the word Ampleforth, I had learnt, was never used by Ampleforth boys; instead, you always talked of SHAC – Senior House, Ampleforth College). To illustrate his point he told us a story. A fifteen-year-old boy had taken the bus to Scarborough on a Saturday afternoon, which was his right, and had found his way into a pub where he had ordered a brandy and soda, which was not. While he was enjoying his drink, a school monitor had come into the pub, rather taking the edge off the moment.

'I suppose you know I'm going to have to have you thrashed,' said the monitor.

'Of course,' came the reply. 'But now that we've got that out of the way, can I buy you a drink?'

That, we were told, was the SHAC spirit. We should observe it at all times and on no account should we become ten-percenters, members of that proportion of the school that persistently showed itself 'bloody-minded and cynical', skulked around with hair uncut and shoes unpolished, and failed to cheer the school at First XV matches. And with that, Whitehead hand-ed over the stage to the school pop group – The Bletch in the Middle Distance. The ear-shattering wall of sound that followed anticipated, by some decades, the emergence of industrial grind-core bands like Nine-Inch Nails. We were a captive audience, but not an unappreciative one.

The school was divided into houses of sixty boys, each with a distinctive character bestowed by its housemaster. There were houses for the tweedily aristocratic, houses for the brainy, houses for the aesthetically inclined. St Edward's, into which I was going, was tough and egalitarian. Its particular distinction was cross-country; we were expected to run every day that we were not playing games.

We shared a building – a modernist edifice designed by Sir Giles Gilbert-Scott and known to us as the Jam Factory – with another house, St Wilfred's, and were very much Sparta to their Athens. They considered us brutish, we thought them effete; the sculptor Antony Gormley and the actor Rupert Everett were both St Wilfred's boys. One of the St Edward's traditions was that senior members of the house brewed beer in one of the house's four baths every Monday and drank it at the following Sunday lunch. Like everyone else, I looked forward to the day when I would be allowed a glass. When the moment finally came, three years later, I discovered what should have been obvious all along: the stuff was all but undrinkable. You swigged it down, despite its lingering aftertaste of shampoo and iron filings, because you could.

It wasn't until the summer term that I visited the Ampleforth lakes. The Prior, Father Anthony, was in charge of the fishing club, which met weekly in one of the classrooms. Following directions on the main school noticeboard, I peered hesitantly through the door and discovered a fly-tying session in progress. The Prior welcomed me, led me to a fly-tying vice and suggested I start with a Black Gnat – supposedly an easy fly to tie. After a time, I became aware that I was being watched. The spectators were a second-year St Edward's boy named Phil and a fair-haired figure I didn't recognize.

'Interesting!' murmured the fair-haired boy. 'A gnat with three wings.'

'The feather sort of split,' I admitted.

They nodded. 'You're a fisherman, then,' said Phil.

'I've done some,' I said carefully.

They looked at each other. 'We're going to the lakes on Saturday,' said Phil. 'If you feel like coming?'

I didn't need asking twice. We met on the road outside the Jam Factory at midday, after the week's final lesson. We all had bicycles, mine a temporary loan in exchange for a bar of Cadbury's milk chocolate from the school shop. Our rods were tied to our crossbars and our fishing-bags were slung over our shoulders. The fair-haired boy's name, I had discovered, was Fergus and he was in St Wilfred's.

We peeled off down the hill into the valley, past the rugby pitches, the cricket pavilion and the sports cinder track. It was a bright, windy May day, and it felt wonderful to be free, however briefly, of classrooms and the school timetable. After a quarter of a mile we crossed the brook, a tiny winding stream containing wild trout and grayling, which Robert had spent countless hours pursuing. The track grew rougher, so that our kit rattled in our bags, and soon we were on the road below Gilling Castle, Ampleforth's prep school.

After a few hundred yards we drew level with a farm and its outbuildings.

'You might care to speed up at this point,' Fergus called to me, as he and Phil started to pedal hell for leather, heads down.

I kept up a normal speed, not understanding their urgency, at which point a massive clod of wet mud and manure thumped into the back of my head, all but knocking me from the bike. Steadying myself, I looked round and saw a heavy, baleful figure in dungarees standing in the upper storey of a barn.

'Fook off!' he roared. 'Tha' fookin' College coonts!'

Again, I didn't need asking twice. 'Barry has rather mixed feelings about us SHAC types,' Fergus explained, as I drew level.

Five minutes' more pedalling took us to the lakes. First the main lake, a substantial body of water where the school Sea Scouts conducted elaborate activities with ropes and pulleys, and where Robert had caught his great pike. Then, at the end of a flinty track, to two much smaller waters fed by a stream. The lower one, a dark panel set amongst high banks of rhododendron, was immediately enticing and a trout showed at the surface even as we climbed from our bikes. The upper lake was wilder and reed-fringed. Apart from a few small birches parading on one bank, it was open to the elements, its surface habitually blown into a purplish chop.

'Which is it to be, Mr Jennings?' asked Fergus genially, waving a proprietorial arm over the scene. The trout, he told me, were hard fished for on both lakes and cunning in consequence.

I opted for the upper lake. The lower was prettier, but with all that rhododendron the casting was likely to be harder. The upper was clear of foliage so if I positioned myself with the wind at my back, I might have a chance of getting out a decent length of line. No matter that tactically speaking this was precisely the wrong thing to do. On a still water you go to the lee shore and cast into the wind, because that's where the insects are blown, and the fish follow the insects. Right now, though, I wasn't worried about catching fish, I was worried about making an arse of myself.

The others opted for the lower lake, so I set up my rod, left it on the bank with my bag and went to watch them. As I'd guessed, they were both very good. Phil spent most of his holidays in South America, catching peacock bass in the steamy rainforests of Guyana. Fergus's family had been posted to the rather drier locale of Addis Ababa in Ethiopia, from where he conducted sorties after Nile perch. Both had landed huge fish in their fourteen or fifteen years on the planet, but both were also entranced by the subtle protocols of catching English brown trout on the fly.

Nothing was rising on the top lake, so I put on a wet fly, a tiny beetle-like thing called a Coch-y-bondhu. I had been fishing this without success for an hour when Fergus appeared and beckoned to me. Phil was into a good fish. It had taken a Black Gnat, fished dry, and he was landing it when we got there. As soon as it was on the bank and knocked on the head, the two of them shouldered their bags and led me into the rhododendrons. In a small clearing, well away from the bank, Phil gutted the trout with a pocket knife, buried the guts, assembled a portable fish smoker and lit the tray of hickory wood chips. From his seemingly bottomless fishing-bag came a quarter-bottle of Smirnoff and cans of Schweppes Bitter Lemon.

'Turban?' enquired Fergus, taking out his tin.

Turban was SHAC-speak for Old Holborn cigarette-rolling tobacco. I didn't smoke when I went to the school, but I was soon experimenting; there was a tobacco culture there to equal any Pall Mall club. At sixteen, after two years in the dormitory, you were allotted a room in which you were allowed, at certain times, to smoke a pipe. This rule, hallowed by time, subverted housemasters' best efforts to safeguard their charges' health. Father Edward must have found it particularly frustrating, as his personal code demanded that he knock and wait for a tactful period before entering any pupil's room. When he did, he as often as not walked into a fug like that of an opium den. In one corner would be the room's sixth-form owner, benignly wreathed in smoke from an elaborately carved meerschaum or calabash, while up to eight other boys sat around in attitudes of studied innocence, their gazes fixed on the Indian wall-hangings and Jimi Hendrix posters.

Not many people people smoked cigarettes; almost everyone

rolled Turban. It was cheaper, it tasted better, and there weren't the giveaway clouds of smoke. Even in the junior years, a startling percentage of the boys were addicted, constantly pleading diarrhoea in class in order to sneak a quick drag in the Crystal Palaces, as the malodorous galleries of lavatory stalls were known. Some made considerable sacrifices of dignity for their habit. Smoking was a beatable offence, but popular wisdom held it that you couldn't be beaten for homosexuality. So truly desperate boys took to smoking in the Upper or Lower Crystal in pairs, so that in the event of a raid by a school monitor, they had an alibi. The ensuing drama tended to play out as follows:

SHAC MONITOR: What the hell are you two turds doing in the same crapper?

FIRST SCROFULOUS YOUTH: I'd rather not say, Arbuthnot. It's personal.

SHAC MONITOR: I'll make it personal, you little shag. Empty out your pockets.

(*A body search of both boys fails to reveal evidence of smoking equipment. Unsurprisingly, since they brought with them only two roll-ups and a single Swan Vesta match.*)

SHAC MONITOR: You both stink of smoke. I'm reporting you to your housemasters.

SECOND SY: Can I tell you something in confidence, Arbuthnot?

SHAC Monitor (*suspiciously*): Spit it out.

Second SY: I was actually tossing Weevil off.

(*Silence*)

First SY: We can't help ourselves, Arbuthnot. We're slaves to the habit.

SHAC Monitor (*less sure of his ground*): If that's true, you should be ashamed of yourselves.

Second SY (*penitently*): You're right. We could both go blind. We were going to speak to Matron about it.

SHAC Monitor (*wearily considering his options, and aware that First XI net practice begins in ten minutes*): Look, you foul little perverts, just bugger off, OK?

There was a clear distinction between Crystal Palace desperadoes and social smokers like Phil and Fergus. Turban-smokers usually kept their works in a two-ounce sealable tin. This was customized by scraping off all the paint, leaving cryptic hieroglyphs that would identify the owner to his peers, but not, obviously, to the authorities. As a frequent airline passenger, Fergus had access to duty-free wares. As a result, his elaborately engraved tin contained a choice of Old Holborn and Golden Virginia tobaccos, each with a twist of apple peel to keep it moist, and a choice of Rizla papers (regular, fine and licorice). This richness of choice seemed more reminiscent of the eighteenth than the twentieth century. After appropriate gestures of gratitude I settled back against a tree trunk with a roll-up in one hand and a fizzing tooth-mug of booze in the other.

'What d'you think, boy?' asked Fergus, as the fish smoker hissed away.

'Pretty good,' I said. And it was. Boarding schools get a bad rap these days, but they certainly offered intensity of experience. I can taste that meal even now.

After lunch we fished together on the lower lake. By then I had got my hand in sufficiently not to make too much of a fool of myself, although it was clear who was the novice of the party. Other fishermen had arrived in the meantime, including the Prior, who wandered around, watching us and smiling cryptically when our flies were ignored by the trout. By late afternoon a couple more fish had been caught, yet most of us had landed nothing. Fergus was right; it was hard fishing.

At about four-thirty, I was back on the top lake with Phil. The light was going and the ride back to the school uphill all the way. To get back to the house, change and make it to the Abbey Church in time for six o'clock Benediction would take about seventy-five minutes. An hour, cut to the bone.

'Show me your fly box,' Phil said, and pointed to a small local fly, a Partridge and Orange, which I'd bought at the fishing club meeting three days earlier.

'Out there.' He nodded, indicating a jagged line of chop, where two wind currents met. It was at the limit of my casting range, but I managed it. On the third offering, a fish hit the fly confidently, streaking for the deep water by the dam as I brought the rod up. Phil watched with arms folded as I played and landed the trout – a handsome three-quarter-pounder with a golden belly and a proliferation of red spots, as well as a good fish for the water. I felt relief and gratitude: I was one of those who had caught, not just a duffer who'd been brought along for the ride.

I thanked Phil for his help, but he waved my words away. 'You learnt to fish with Nairac, didn't you?'

I nodded. I had no idea how he knew.

'Everyone said he was a good Head of House,' said Phil. 'And an unbelievable fisherman.'

Old Amplefordians tended to be talked of like that by those still doing their time at SHAC. In the past tense, as if they were dead.

FIFTEEN

OVER THAT SUMMER AND THOSE THAT FOLLOWED, I returned to the lakes many times. I got to know every yard of the route: the long downhill run past the pavilion and the cinder track, the brief flash of the brook, the dismal slog through the outlying rugby pitches, the gauntlet-run past the farm, the final push on foot up the flinty path. And always that billowing, wind-in-the-sails sense of freedom after the endless classes, the communal meals, the grinding runs, the ill-organized games, the pointless boot-polishing and drilling of the cadet corps.

I caught fish from time to time, but more often I didn't, and the same went for everyone who fished there. We were a small group; whatever the differences of year and seniority during the week, on the lakes we were equal. An unspoken rule demanded that monitors put aside their authority while fishing, which most were happy to do: anyone standing on his dignity under such circumstances would have looked pretty silly.

I took to carrying around a matchbox with basic fly-tying equipment in it: a handful of Size 14 and 16 hooks, a few hackle feathers, a miniature spool of silk and tying thread. In a dull class, if you were discreet, you could assemble a perfectly serviceable dry fly. In my first year I learnt French with a venerable teacher named Monsieur Cossart. A figure of unfathomable antiquity, tiny and birdlike in his black gown, he had been my father's French teacher in the mid-1930s and fairly ancient even then.

'Jumping Ted', as he was sometimes called, was a demon for grammar and, in particular, the subjunctive mood. In twelve months of classes I don't remembering him broaching any other subject except once, when he decided to brush up our general culture, getting one of the assistants to bring in his magic lantern and a box of glass slides showing famous French views. There, in cracked sepia, was Nice's Promenade des Anglais, with *boulevardiers* in blazers and boaters sauntering past the Hôtel Negresco. There, projected upside down, was the Rue de la Paix and the Opéra de Paris.

Cossart had written a French Grammar, yet we only ever studied one part of it: Section 21C, which dealt with his beloved subjunctive. To fail to master this mood, he implied, was not only to do poorly in our O levels but at some profound level to fail as a human being. He would constantly cite the example of a former student who had disdained the teachings of Section 21C. 'And what is he doing now?' Cossart would demand with a

Gallic shrug. 'Selling postcards in the Wallace Collection!'

Mindful of this worse-than-death outcome, I applied myself with moderate diligence to Cossart's teachings. I always used to sit at the same desk in his class; there was a very useful crack in the side into which, like a vice, you could jam the bend of a hook as you applied the silk body and hackle feather. Jumping Ted's eyes were not what they'd been before the Treaty of Versailles, and a couple of books on the desk would effectively conceal the operation.

I certainly wouldn't have tried any such thing in Mr Macbean's French Literature class. This dramatically inclined Scotsman, with a pompadour of silver hair, would rake the class with a gaze of hawklike intensity as he recited exquisitely modulated passages of Corneille or Racine. He had a particular affinity for the role of Andromaque. Sweeping the tail of his gown over one shoulder, eyes blazing beneath the winter surf of his coiffure, he would tilt back his head and, like some great heroine of the Comédie-Française, declaim of the fall of Troy: 'Songe, songe, Céphise, à cette nuit cruelle, qui fut pour toute un peuple, une nuit éternelle...'

Macbean had served with distinction in one of the Highland regiments, and when we had had enough of French Literature it was fairly easy to nudge him into reminiscence. He always put up a token resistance, but we would have none of it:

Macbean: And so you can see that, in the character of Thérèse Desqueyroux, Mauriac brings us face to face with one of his preoccupying themes: that of sin and redemption. But does he present us with a conclusion? (*Looks around the classroom*) Yes, Willbourne?

Willbourne (*polishing his glasses*): Sir, what was the most Germans you ever killed in one day?

Macbean: Really, Willbourne, I hardly think…

All: Oh go on, sir. Tell us, sir.

Macbean (*modestly, like Shirley Bassey acceding to a request for an encore*): Well…

(*Second pupil runs to corner of classroom and returns with a broom*)

Second pupil: Here's the Bren Gun, Sir.

Macbean: Well, there was an occasion… (*lowers himself to the floor between two lines of desks, braces the broom against his shoulder, checks range*) We'd set up an ambush at a crossroads, waiting for the enemy. Finally the first column appeared…

Third pupil: Did you let them have it straight away, Sir?

Macbean: No, never. You let a few go by. And then, just when they think it's safe… (*thumbs down the safety-catch*) BA-BA-BA-BA-BA-BA-BA-BA-BA-BA-BA-BA-BA-BA-BA-BA-BA!

Initially, I was rather keen on the idea of biology. We hadn't done any science at prep school. While chemistry and physics seemed completely beyond the pale in terms of dullness – I already loathed the world of slide rules and logarithm tables – biology sounded as if it might touch on the things I loved: the outdoor world and the natural order. This naive hope dissolved within minutes of arriving for my first class. Biology was taught in the profoundly sinister Lab 10, which would have made an effective set for a Frankenstein film. The walls were lined with glass jars filled with nameless horrors pickled in brownish formalin, including a twenty-six-foot tapeworm expelled by a pupil in the infirmary. A cloying, sulphurous odour hung over the place, whilst a dim light rose from tanks full of giant cockroaches, retained for experimental purposes. These creatures – a good two inches in length, with long, questing antennae – explored the glass walls of their prisons with a tentative clicking sound. Once one had moved past the initial revulsion, it was hard not to feel a certain solidarity. Like us, they were being prepared for death.

Lab 10 was the domain of a teacher known as Morb. Universally feared, he had a grim and scowling aspect, a choleric temperament and a beating arm like a Cappadocian slave-master. Worse, he had an overriding obsession with sex and specifically with adolescent masturbation. No biological issue was so remote from the sin of Onan that it could not be steered back to it.

We would glance at each other with dread as we approached danger zones like the dispersal of dandelion spores or cell division in spirogyra.

'If I hear the phrase "engorged with blood" once more I'm going to throw myself out of that window,' a friend murmured to me after yet another session on Morb's Special Subject.

He was, in short, very nearly mad, and any chance to escape his classes was seized with alacrity. Such a chance came the way of my cousin Julian and me when, following some large-scale dissection, we were asked to get rid of the heart and lungs of an ox. We dragged them out of Lab 10 in a plastic dustbin – the organs sloshing around in a gallon or so of fetid blood – and made for the scientific waste disposal area, which was just outside the school tuck shop. We were just about to perform the task as requested when we saw a novice monk approaching in the distance. The same thought occurred to both of us at the same time, and as Julian bent double over the dustbin, retching theatrically, I stared around me wildly.

'Brother James,' I gasped as he approached. 'Dawson's just vomited, and rather a lot's come up…'

He looked at me suspiciously as Julian, head lolling, put in a convincing groan. A single glance at the bloody horror in the dustbin was enough. The young monk went white as a sheet and stared at Julian open-mouthed. It was probably not the best moment for me to snigger, nor for Julian to snort with laughter.

It would have been hard to count just how many school rules we were contravening at that instant. Brother James, however, took the deceit in good part and decided not to report us to our respective housemasters. He demonstrated SHAC spirit.

The Catholic Church has an association with fishing dating back to mediaeval times, when monasteries and abbeys had their own lakes and stew ponds, in which pike, bream, carp and other species were reared for the table. The first English reference to fishing occurs in the *Colloquium* of Aelfric, Abbott of Eynsham, at the end of the tenth century. In 1496 the pursuit was described in much greater detail in the *Treatyse of Fysshynge with an Angle*, ascribed to Dame Juliana Berners, an abbess of St Albans. Mediaeval illustrations show monks fishing in fresh water with rod and line, and it's reasonable to assume that fishing skills were passed down through the religious orders.

But has angling, with its profoundly metaphorical character, ever really been a wholly appropriate pursuit for those subject to Catholic vows of poverty, chastity and obedience? One senses, in those watery demesnes outside the mediaeval abbey walls, the presence of the Fisher King of the Grail Romances, and the Arthurian Lady of the Lake. This ambiguity was nicely expressed in a risqué Edwardian postcard I once saw, which showed a party of Friar Tucks staring with guilty delight at a well-endowed mermaid they had landed.

By the time I was at Ampleforth, only one or two of the older monks fished, a fact I found obscurely disappointing. At the time very few ex-Amplefordians were going into the monastery, and it seemed to me that the new liturgy was at least partly responsible. Liberalization had been achieved at the expense of grandeur and mystery, which had put off more traditionally minded applicants. Their place was being taken by younger, hipper monks-to-be from outside the establishment, many of them prepared to countenance an almost limitless elasticity of belief. I remember one recent arrival crossing the monastery car park in a swish of cassocks; as he passed me he winked and sketched out a blessing, crooning the words 'Dominus Vobiscum' to the tune of 'I Wanna be Bobby's Girl'.

Amongst the boys, existentialism was a fashionable posture, usually accessorized by a loose tie, a worn paperback copy of Sartre's *Nausée* and a studied air of anomie. But what really agitated the younger monks, I discovered, was to express a taste for the more gothic aspects of Catholicism: for physical relics and *ex voto* offerings, levitating saints, statues that wept blood, animals that fell to their knees and worshipped their Saviour, and fish that bore the marks of the Holy Wounds. For progressive Catholics, post-Vatican Two, such things were anathema, and the mere mention of phenomena such as miracle cures or demonic possession was enough to freak them into contortions of defensive rationalism. Backsliders they knew how to deal with; it was enthusiasts that genuinely alarmed them.

My favourite teacher was Algy Haughton, who taught English. An urbane and stylish figure with a darkly ironic manner, he would listen to any argument if it was well expressed, and was happy – in absolute defiance of school rules – to continue the discussion in the pub on a Saturday afternoon. A couple of hours would put paid to any notion of fishing that day – with three or four pints of Tadcaster Bitter on board, there was no question of riding a bicycle in a straight line, let alone attaching and casting a tiny dry fly – but it was worth it. Algy was of a fatalistic bent and his disquisitions on *Hamlet*, in particular, were thrilling: real breakneck rides through the dark night of the soul. He turned the same mordant gaze on *Measure for Measure*, *The Revenger's Tragedy* and *The Caretaker*, elegantly dissecting each layer of meaning. When it was announced that the annual school play would be *Edward II* and that Algy would be directing it, I auditioned immediately. I had no talent whatever for speaking verse but guessed, correctly, that he would bring Marlowe's drama to murderously suggestive life. Whilst my own part was short on speech, it was satisfyingly packed with lurid and violent action.

In return for his attention, and those beery, smoke-wreathed afternoons in the Malt Shovel at Oswaldkirk, Algy expected a lot. When I complained that we were being made to study writers whose work was banal and superficial, he forced me to make my case line by line, savagely dismissing my jejune generalizations and forcing me into a genuinely critical posture. Although I wasn't by a long chalk his cleverest pupil, I was one of the most combative, and I think that amused him.

Another literature teacher, a Wildean figure named Ian Davie who had been encouraged as a young poet by Siegfried Sassoon, ran a parallel literary court in The Grange, a house in the school grounds. Here he dispensed white wine and gentle advice as aspiring Shelleys read out their verse. Although no poet myself, I was asked along to one such meeting, whose atmosphere I found a bit coy after literary sparring sessions with Algy. In the classroom Ian could be eloquent on the subject of heterosexual love but, as we quickly discovered, preferred to keep the whole thing safely abstract:

> IAN: Of course, on the night that he married her, Othello would have discovered whether Desdemona was a virgin.
> (*The class digests this information in silence. Ian winces, realizing the Pandora's Box that he has opened.*)
> FIRST PUPIL (*with deliberation*): How, sir, exactly?
> IAN : Well, he would have… (*flutters fingers uncomfortably*) Look, ask your biology teachers, OK?
> SECOND PUPIL (*helpfully*): We dissected the vulva of a rat this morning.
> IAN (*faintly, closing eyes*): Oh God…

Algy, by contrast, was always happy to engage with brute physicality, especially on stage, and *Edward II* gets very brutal indeed.

I remember long discussions in the green room – Algy with a cigarette in his hand and a wry half-smile on his face – as we discussed the mechanics of assassination, with diversions into the mystery of Marlowe's own death in a Deptford tavern. Algy's wife Rosemary was often present, sewing costumes. A dark-eyed figure in gypsyish skirts, she was a radical theologian and much-published author, whose presence added to the sense of the theatre as a place apart.

In a world of rules and timetables, that dusty Aladdin's cave of a green room represented all that was mysterious and heart-quickening. As Algy's domain, it became a locus of glamour, danger and transformation. He was the best kind of literature teacher, in that he left you to make your own discoveries. He didn't lead you in – just took you close enough to see the light streaming under the door. Only with the distance of years can I see what I owe him.

SIXTEEN

Winters at SHAC could be austere. There was pike-fishing on the main lake, in which the odd fish of three or four pounds succumbed to my Colorado Spoon, although I never came close to anything approaching Robert's fifteen-pounder. In the autumn, when the cold really started to bite, I'd go out after grayling in the brook, trotting tiny red worms downstream beneath a toothpick float cocked by a single dust-shot. It was hard fishing, yielding only one or two in an entire afternoon, but it was oddly satisfying to fish on the boundaries of the school rugby pitches, moving unseen between the banks as the Under-16 Colts battled Barnard Castle or Sedburgh in the mist.

In the summer, though, the valley came to life. As the days lengthened, the muddy hillsides that we'd pounded all winter shed their dismal aspect, revealing banks of violet and celandine, and slopes whitened with sharp-scented wild garlic. On school holidays the Prior would load a half-dozen of us into a school minibus and drive us out to Stonegrave, or Farndale, or some other stretch of moorland trout-water. My memory of these occasions, which I would look forward to for weeks, is that the sun always shone. Those little limestone streams, winding their unhurried way through the North Yorkshire dales, were some of the loveliest waters I've ever fished. We used the local wet flies – Snipe and Purple, Partridge and Orange – casting them upstream and across, so that they swept under the deep grassy overhangs. You struck when you saw the flash of a turning fish, at which point, if you were lucky, you'd feel the jinking run of a trout, or the nervy flutter of a grayling. They were rarely big – a half-pounder was a respectable fish – but they were beautiful: the trout dark-backed and spotted with scarlet, the grayling lit with a purplish shimmer.

The day would end with the first fading of the light, and with Benediction: lines of boys streaming from their houses to the Abbey Church through the summer-scented evening. The service would begin with a procession of monks, spectral in their black cowls, taking their places behind the altar to the sound of twelfth-century plainchant. Kneeling there, with the pleasing sting of sunburn on the back of my neck and the faint smell of thyme on my hands from unhooking grayling (the Romans called them *thymalli*), I would meditate on the day's fishing. If it had been a particularly good day, there would be a trout for supper. As head of St Edward's House, before he went on to become Head of School, Robert had established the principle that fisherman were allowed to have their catches cooked and served to them.

He visited SHAC a couple of times when I was there. By then he was at Oxford, reading History and captaining the university boxing club. The last time he came up, it was a weekday. Normally I would have been confined to the school buildings, but Robert persuaded Father Edward to give me permission to fish the evening rise on the brook. We drove to the east of the valley, parked the car and walked through still-warm fields marked with the hoof imprints of cattle. Pigeons flew over us, cresting the roadside trees with a single wing-snap and gliding to their roosts. The tiny stream was heavily overgrown, the water just an occasional gleam beneath overhanging bushes.

'Doesn't look like anyone's fished the place since I was last here,' said Robert, as he set up the six-foot Hardy rod. I made up a short tapered leader and attached a John Storey, a local dry fly with a speckled white mallard wing. Then we stepped down into the water in our tennis shoes and, as quietly as we could, crept upstream.

It was precision fishing, probably the most exacting I've ever done. Most of the time we were in deep shadow, crouching beneath a roof of foliage only occasionally pierced with light. The stream was rarely more than six feet wide; a pool might be a foot deep. We took it in turns to cast, flicking the little dry fly a rod's length ahead, watching intently as it rode the miniature currents back to us on its curving white wing. There was the odd rise, but mostly we were fishing speculatively, casting to where we thought fish might lie.

After a quarter of an hour we saw a trout come up to the surface a couple of pools ahead, taking a live insect with the confident, slashing take of a fish who knows himself lord of his domain. As we edged closer, sliding our feet noiselessly through the water, it rose again. The pool was dark, shot through with amber shafts of light, and the trout was stationed at its head. I was holding the rod, crouching on the right-hand side of the stream. To cover the fish would take a near-impossible backhand cast, so I held the butt out to Robert, at which he grinned and shook his head. I cursed him – I was certain to screw this one up – but he flashed me a V-sign and jerked his thumb upstream.

Kneeling in the water, I drew off some line and took the fly between two fingers. Braking the reel-drum, I pulled the leader taut against the bend of the rod and sighted along the split-cane as if it were a catapult. I let go, the line flicked straight, the leader turned over, and the fly dropped to the head of the pool. Nothing happened for a moment, then the surface bulged and the fly disappeared – at which point I pulled the hook straight out of the trout's mouth. I groaned, furious with myself for having wasted that amazing fluke of a cast. Striking too soon was the cardinal dry-fly sin; the mark of the overexcited beginner. Morosely, I picked the sodden John Storey from my hair, where it had come to rest, and blew it dry.

Robert, however, was staring upstream, eyes narrowed.

'I think he's still there,' he murmured. 'I don't think he felt it.'

I followed his gaze, and could just see the faint bow-wave of the circling fish. I handed him the rod and this time he took it. Kneeling down in the water once more, I pressed myself as far back as I could against the overhanging bush. The line hissed past my face as Robert cast. The fish ignored the first drift of the fly, but came up to the second with another of those confident, slashing takes. He went a little over the half-pound, a beautiful wild fish.

By the time bad light forced us to stop and we climbed out on to the bank – cut, scratched, nettle-stung, soaked to mid-thigh – we had three trout in the bag, all caught by Robert. I'd managed a few decent casts, but it hadn't been my night. It had, on the other hand, been a master class in dry-fly fishing under conditions most would have dismissed as impossible, and any time spent with Robert was a good time.

We lit cigarettes on the bank and he told me about Oxford. The social life was good – parties, Pimm's, May balls and the rest of it. There had been trouble, though. He'd been followed home one night by four skinheads, who'd jeered at him as a toff. The usual town–gown hostility. They'd surrounded him and asked whether he wanted a fight, to which he'd naturally said yes, and put all four of them in hospital. Whilst this had not been regarded favourably by the authorities, he'd got away with a warning.

I knew him well enough to detect an oblique note to this story. Robert was not a particularly big guy, but he was tough-looking, and held himself like a fighter. He was the very last person, in a city of bookish types, that the average gang of boneheads would have picked on, and at some level, I felt sure, he'd provoked the fight. There was more, Robert continued. He'd taken LSD, admitted it to the Lincoln College authorities, and been sent down for a term, although he'd managed to keep the affair quiet. Luckily, he was to be allowed to continue his studies. He hoped to join the Army.

I was surprised by the LSD. This was 1970, and drugs were everywhere, but it seemed out of character. Forty years later, following the publication of the first edition of this book, I was told by the novelist Duncan Fallowell, who knew Robert at Oxford, that I was almost certainly mistaken about the sending-down. In March 2011, however, I was approached by Richard Lowden, another Oxford contemporary, who remembered Robert turning up at his lodgings in Keble College at 3 am, white-faced and shaking after a bad trip, saying that he'd seen The Devil. Even in the cold light of the following day, Lowden told me, Robert was so convinced of the evil that he'd encountered that he'd reported all those involved to the authorities, heedless of the consequences to his own career. No one else who knew about this incident has ever spoken out. In a biography of Robert published in 1999, John Parker quotes Julian Malins QC:

The Oxford class of '68 was good-looking, confident and unlike any previous generation since the 1930s. We came after austerity and before the shadow of stress had fallen on the young. We parked our cars on Radcliffe Square. We dined at the Elizabeth. The sun shone and the girls were sensational. Work was not on the agenda. In this third year, Robert's car was stolen and though it was recovered, his history notes had mysteriously disappeared. Of course, the Rector of Lincoln allowed him a fourth year… It was the Swinging Sixties. Even against such a backdrop, Robert stood out. He was the most handsome of his generation. He had a terrific aura. No one could be in his presence without feeling better for it. That is a great and rare gift.

Malins's words ring true. They reflect, with sincerity, Robert's extraordinary charisma. But there's something else there, something which Malins loyally waves away even as he records it. A sense of a life not fully in control. The business of the stolen car and the 'mysteriously' vanished notes occurred the year after the skinhead fight and the LSD affair. Together, they give the impression of something troubling stirring beneath the sunlit surface. Robert joined the Grenadier Guards, Malins's family providing the necessary introductions, and spent his final year at Oxford in uniform. The waters closed over the earlier incidents.

Squelching back to the car in our wet shoes, we drove to a

nearby pub. With our pints set up before us, Robert announced that he had fresh trout to give away. Soon we were surrounded by smiling faces and he was telling stories, eliciting roars of laughter, handshakes and slaps on the back. Pubs were Robert's theatre. I saw him, time and time again, walk into a bar, grinning that easy grin, undaunted by the silence provoked by the entry of a stranger. Within minutes, he'd have the place at his feet. He was at once the maverick toff, the life-and-soul raconteur, the poacher with a pocket full of trout. And while no one completely believed in these personae, everyone at some level wanted to, because they seemed to stand for the old values and better times. All of this was less a matter of calculation – although calculation did enter into it – than of instinct. He wanted to make people feel good around him and he knew just how to do it. Later, there would be those who would express reservations about his need for centre-stage visibility and approbation. But that was later.

Shortly after breakfast the next day a car horn sounded on the road outside the Jam Factory. It was Robert, and he was moving on. As I went down the steps, he leant out of the car and skimmed something towards me through the air. It was a flat green tin, printed with the words 'The Loch Leven Eyed Fly Box'. Inside were rows of hand-tied dry flies: Mayflies, Ginger Quills, Red Spinners, Blue-Winged Olives, Iron-Blue Duns and Black Gnats. I looked up. He grinned, waved and was gone.

SEVENTEEN

J. W. DUNNE IS REMEMBERED BY ANGLERS FOR HIS BOOK *Sunshine and the Dry Fly*, but there was a time when he had a wider following. Born into the Anglo-Irish aristocracy in 1875, Dunne fought in the Boer War before becoming a pioneer of aircraft design, creating a series of tailless, swept-wing biplanes that were taken up by the US Army. Alongside this work, and his investigations on the chalk streams, he pursued another, more abstract field of enquiry.

In 1902, Dunne dreamt of the eruption of Mount Pelée in Martinique, the actual event occurring several days later. A series of other such precognitive dreams followed. They led, following twenty-five years of practical experimentation, to the publication of *An Experiment with Time* (1927) and *The Serial Universe* (1934), in which Dunne argued that linear time is an illusion, and that past, present and future are in fact simultaneous. We experience them sequentially only because of the limits of our consciousness, limits that dissolve in the dream-state. With death, Dunne continued in *The New Immortality* (1938), we fall out of time altogether and into eternity.

I don't think it's insignificant, in all of this, that Dunne was a fisherman. Rivers, by their nature, incline one to thoughts of time and its flow. Had T. S. Eliot read Dunne when he wrote, in the opening lines of 'Burnt Norton':

> Time present and time past
> Are both perhaps present in time future
> And time future contained in time past.

Certain landscapes are resonant with this possibility: with the sense of a confluence of the personal, temporal and historical. They stop you in your tracks, and behind your breastbone something expands in a space too tight to contain it. There's sadness, but consolation too, and of the two the consolation is the greater.

The last time I felt these things was not in the countryside, but in the Capodimonte Museum in Naples. I had been wandering rather absently round the gallery when I suddenly came face to face with a painting of extraordinary, shimmering beauty. Claude Lorrain's *Landscape with the Nymph Egeria* was painted for Prince Lorenzo Colonna and completed in 1669. Its theme is taken from Book XV of Ovid's *Metamorphoses*, which tells the story of the second, semi-mythical king of Rome, Numa Pompilius. After Numa's death, his widow, the water nymph Egeria, leaves Rome and hides herself 'in the deep woods that grow in the valley of Aricia'. There, her lamentations disturb the worshippers at the nearby temple of Diana. The goddess's nymphs beseech Egeria to restrain her tears but she is inconsolable. Eventually, moved by her grief, Diana turns her into a freshwater stream.

The painting, which is more than six feet long, contains at least twenty figures, but these are rendered almost insignificant by the scale of the landscape. We see a pretty, fair-haired Egeria in the foreground, surrounded by four of Diana's nymphs, identifiable by their bows, spears and dogs. One of the nymphs is kneeling beside Egeria, pointing to the temple in the valley as if to say: 'Please! We can hear you almost half a mile away!' Another pair, having clearly given up on Egeria, are making their way back to the valley, chatting. Above them, on a promontory, stands a single column – the heraldic device of the Colonna family. The temple, pillared and grand, is far below them in the valley and lapping its steps is a broad waterway, with boats. We know from Claude's drawings that this was based on Lake Nemi, known in antiquity as 'the mirror of Diana', on whose northern shores the Colonna family owned property, including the castle that in the picture stands on a promontory beyond the temple. Here, however, it doesn't look like a lake; it looks more like a river with steep wooded banks.

The elegiac mood of the painting is conveyed through the shadowed browns and olives of the woods in the foreground and the ruined castle against the sky. The wider landscape, in contrast, is bathed in the transparent light of evening. The woods on the far bank are a silvery green, the water a soft, deep blue. There's sadness – this is a painting about death, after all – but there's also consolation. And there's something else, something which, that day in Naples, I couldn't quite identify. I stood in front of it until we had to leave, but it was only later that I realized what it was. Not only does the lake look like a river; it looks like a river that flows inland, winding its way from the horizon and coming to a halt at the steps of the temple. This, Claude seems to say, is the end-place, and here there is no time. The Colonna castle under-lines the point. Numa Pompilius died in the seventh century BC, but the castle, which would not be built for fifteen hundred years, is already a ruin. Past, present and future are one.

Our lives proceed upstream. The common waterweed of the chalk streams is *Elodea canadensis*. It is easily recognizable by its emerald strands and the tiny white flowers that burst from it in summer. Its other name is egeria.

EIGHTEEN

IT WAS MAY 1977, AND I WAS WORKING IN PERTH, WEST-
ern Australia, when Paul, with whom I'd done so much of my
earliest fishing, sent me a bundle of newspaper cuttings. I took
them outside and read them with the City Beach surf booming
in my ears. Robert had been working undercover in Northern
Ireland and was missing, believed killed.

The first reports were sketchy. It seemed that on Saturday 14
May, he had left a British Army base in South Armagh, saying that
he was going to a nearby bar. He had failed to report back to his
HQ and later that night his car had been found in the car park
outside the bar. There were signs of a violent struggle. After two
days, during which the army and police had mounted a massive
search of the area, the Provisional IRA had announced that
Captain Robert Nairac was dead, executed following interrogation in which he had admitted that he was a member of the
Special Air Service. The lack of a body led many to question the

IRA claims. But two more days later the Irish police reported evidence of an incident in Ravensdale Forest, south of the border. Bullet cases had been found and bloodstains. *Republican News*, an IRA mouthpiece, released a second statement, claiming 'the elimination of Nairac' as a breakthrough in the war against the SAS.

On 28 May, following a tip-off, an IRA terror suspect named Liam Patrick Townson was arrested by the Gardai at a roadblock outside Newry, in the Republic. North of the border the Royal Ulster Constabulary arrested a further five men. Townson confessed almost immediately to Robert's murder. He had been drinking in a pub, he said, when he had been summoned to Ravensdale and told to bring a gun. He had found a captive who, following hours of interrogation, 'was in a bad state'. Unable to extract any information, he had shot him.

Robert's abductors, it turned out, were low-level IRA sympathizers. Their amateurism was shown by the fact that, having snatched someone they thought was a British soldier, they hadn't contacted their superiors on the Army Council. Robert was high on the IRA's wanted list and his capture would have been a huge propaganda coup. Instead, his kidnappers had killed him without even discovering his name. It was rumoured that the IRA themselves, furious at this lost opportunity, had turned in Townson and the others.

A year later, on the anniversary of Robert's death, I attended a memorial service at the Guards Chapel in Birdcage Walk, at which Father Edward officiated alongside army clergy. I went alone and sat beneath a window engraved with a falcon in Robert's memory. When it was over, I spoke briefly to his distraught parents and then walked through the thin spring sunshine towards Sloane Square. Somewhere along the way I passed a pub, bought a drink and carried it outside to the pavement. I found myself, out of the blue, remembering an occasion a dozen years earlier at a prep-school sports day. After the speeches and the prize-giving, I came across Robert leaning against the trunk of a large cedar, grinning to himself. He told me that earlier in the day he'd been asked to look out for a couple who were due to arrive at teatime to help with the catering, and to direct them to the kitchens. A couple had turned up at the appointed hour and in accented English asked him where they should go, at which point he had set them to work. For an hour or so, assuming that they were conforming to some eccentric English notion of 'mucking in', a senior Latin American diplomat and his wife had prepared plates of strawberries and ice cream. All things considered, Robert said, the couple had taken it 'pretty well' when the real caterers had turned up.

While some of Robert's activities in Northern Ireland have become a matter of public record, others will probably always remain secret. Enigmatic details have leaked out over the last three decades, but even today much of the story remains unknown, buried in army and Security Services records, as well as in the memories of those who will never talk of it. I've tried, neverthe-less, to patch together an account of those years from the handful of available sources.

Robert served his first tour of duty in the province as a Grenadier Guardsman in 1973, involving himself with 'hearts and minds' initiatives, and teaching boxing at local youth clubs – the kind of activity at which he excelled. When the battalion returned to London, he volunteered for special duties in the Province, rather than accompanying his colleagues to Hong Kong. He wanted, he said, to make a contribution. He was sent on a number of Intelligence courses, one of them run by the SAS in Hereford, geared to operations in Northern Ireland. In 1974, as the Troubles entered their bloodiest decade, he became a liaison officer between various covert Army Intelligence units and the RUC Special Branch in South Armagh. Again, this was a role in which he proved highly adept.

At the same time, to the consternation of many of his col-leagues, he started visiting Republican bars in the area. There, adopting an Irish accent and with his dog at his side, he would engage prominent Republicans in conversation, sing rebel songs and otherwise cultivate a highly visible profile. Was this just an extreme form of intelligence-gathering? Hiding in plain sight, so as to allay suspicion? Or was he playing a longer game, trail-ing his coat past IRA high-ups in the hope of actually being recruited? Both courses would have been suicidally dangerous;

neither was by any stretch of the imagination within the remit of a liaison officer.

Years later, as a journalist, I was taught foot-following and surveillance techniques by a former Northern Ireland undercover operative, who described to me the gnawing stress and fear involved with merely being on the streets in Republican areas, knowing that at any moment you could be dragged into a car and driven away for brutal interrogation, probably followed by a 'head-job'. It was a terrifying environment, and to behave as Robert behaved would have taken exceptional courage. Was he, as some believe, answering to a higher Intelligence authority than the Army? Had he, as many now believed, been recruited by the Security Services? Martin Dillon, the former BBC journalist whose book *The Dirty War* is regarded by many as the authoritative account of the period, quotes an RUC source who describes a meeting with Robert and 'an old man from London' whom Dillon took to be Maurice Oldfield of MI6-SIS or Peter Wright of MI5. If Robert was working for one or other of these Services, it would explain why no apparent control was placed on his freelance activities, then or later.

There are other, less conspiratorial, possibilities. Robert, as all who knew him would agree, was in thrall to certain uncompromising notions of how life should be lived. He was a professed admirer of T. E. Lawrence, and as an Amplefordian of his era he would also have been familiar with the diaries of Hugh Dormer, an old boy of the school who was decorated for his exploits with the Special Operations Executive (reading Shakespeare's *Henry V* in the aircraft that dropped him in France) and killed in action in 1944. By the time I was in the school, Dormer had become, as Robert himself would become, an Amplefordian ideal: that of the brave Catholic soldier prepared to die for a cause. In St Edward's, during the school's annual retreat, the diaries were read to us at meals. 'The sublime moments of sacrifice on the battle-field,' Dormer wrote, 'must bind men together into eternity.'

Something of this spirit is detectable in the way that Robert conducted himself in Northern Ireland. He didn't have a death wish; he enjoyed life and lived it more intensely than anyone I have ever met, but he unquestionably felt the need, in any given situation, to push beyond the formal constraints of his role. To rewrite the narrative, and his own part in it, in romantic and absolutist terms. I would guess that there wasn't a single moment, in the chaos and savagery of those years, when he felt that he was doing less than his duty. However, I would also guess that he sometimes saw this duty differently to those around him. The risk would have been part of that. Part of the business of pushing himself further than anyone else, of daring all.

If Robert's methods sometimes appeared reckless, the knowledge he acquired paid dividends in Intelligence terms. According to a senior staff officer, 'He probably had a better understanding than anyone I met of the IRA, their history and motivations and the Republican cause, along with the communities which supported it.' After his death, however, a number of damaging accusations would surface. It was said that he was part of a unit that was running agents who were members of violent Loyalist groups and helping to set up the murder of Republicans. Given that both sides employed disinformation and black propaganda, and that the records of the units in question are unlikely to be made public any time soon, it is impossible to substantiate these claims. Accusations that Robert was personally involved in two such murders, however, have been comprehensively refuted by Martin Dillon.

In the summer of 1975, Robert returned to Wellington Barracks in London on leave. When he went back to South Armagh in early 1976, it was as a liaison between the RUC Special Branch and the SAS. Whilst Robert was never a 'badged' member of the SAS, as an officer on secondment he was nonetheless bound by their rules. These he consistently flouted and, according to a source quoted by his biographer John Parker, was given to 'wandering around the countryside looking for the IRA at night, or meeting unknown contacts in some godforsaken stretch of terrain, or going into dodgy pubs without back-up'. If on occasion these tactics produced valuable intelligence, his refusal to conform to operational protocol was increasingly resented by the procedure-conscious SAS. Of particular concern was his insistence, alongside his covert activities, on patrolling with regular soldiers. In Crossmaglen, in the heart of 'bandit country', he would walk the streets in uniform, his long hair and pump-action shotgun, a weapon specific to the SAS, telling their own story.

Anyone who has ever gambled knows that you can reach a point where you have the illusion of control, where you think that you can see the patterns governing the turn of the cards or the spin of the wheel. Is this what Robert was beginning to feel? That he could read the underlying structures? That he could see, in his head, how it all fitted together? Had he taken so many risks, and tasted so many adrenalin highs, that the lethally danger-ous just felt ordinary? If the SAS were concerned about his freelance activities, they still needed a knowledgeable liaison offi-cer. No one knew the territory better than Robert did and no one had better contacts in the RUC. As the months passed, and the SAS squadrons were rotated, he remained in place, but the stress was clearly taking its toll. On a leave period in London he told more than one friend that he was working undercover and had infiltrated the IRA.

'They think I'm Irish,' he said. 'One of the boys.'

Julian Malins was amongst those who reacted with disbelief, and tried to persuade him to return to his parent regiment. 'A child could tell from fifty paces that Robert was Ampleforth, Oxford and Guards,' said Malins. 'There never walked a man less capable of deception, let alone anything dishonourable.'

One SAS colonel, recognizing that Robert's erratic behaviour and sense of his own untouchability was an indication that he had been too long in the field, tried to have him pulled out in early 1977, but was told that the liaison officer was needed for 'one more tour'. An RUC Intelligence report came in about the same time, indicating that a local IRA unit was 'going to get' the SAS man called Danny. Robert, who used the cover name Danny McAlevey, laughed off the warning, telling colleagues that he was cultivating an important new source. This, he implied, was the intelligence breakthrough that would change everything. In the first fortnight of May, he went out several times to meet contacts, and received a number of anonymous phone calls.

On Saturday 14 May, he left the SAS HQ at Bessbrook Mill, telling the duty officer that he was going to the Three Steps Inn in Drumintree. Whether he went there as part of a personal initiative, or under orders, is not known. He was dressed in plainclothes and carrying a concealed Browning 9mm handgun. Witnesses noted his entrance to the crowded bar and saw him in conversation with several men. Later in the evening he sang several songs with the band, to loud applause. When he left the pub, however, a number of men were waiting for him and a fierce struggle broke out. Robert managed to get to his car, where he had left the Browning, but was overcome by his captors, disarmed and driven away. He was taken over the border, to a field by a bridge over the River Flurry, and there given a further kicking and beating. Despite severe injuries, he managed to grab back his Browning and get a shot off, hitting one of the kidnappers in the leg before being disarmed again.

When Liam Townson arrived, half drunk, he attempted to interrogate Robert, beating him about the head with his rusty revolver. Robert managed to grab the weapon and turning it on Townson he pulled the trigger. It jammed and he was disarmed for a third time. The subsequent beating with a wooden post left him helpless, lying face down in the field, but he still stuck to his story that he was Danny McAlevey from the Ardoyne, in Belfast.

Knowing that they were going to kill him, Robert asked for a Catholic priest and was given a minute in which to mutter a final prayer. Then Townson levelled his revolver and after three misfires, shot him through the head. Later, a Provisional IRA team would remove his body.

'He never told us anything,' Townson told Irish detectives when arrested a fortnight later. 'He was a great soldier.'

Six men, including Townson, who was sentenced to life, would be imprisoned for their roles in Robert's abduction and killing. Three others went on the run, of whom one, Kevin Crilly, was apprehened by police in County Armagh in 2008 and in November 2009 charged with murder. At the time of writing he awaits trial.

Two years after his death, Robert was awarded the George Cross. His citation ends with the following words: 'Captain Nairac's exceptional courage and acts of the greatest heroism in circumstances of extreme peril showed devotion to duty and personal courage second to none.' His body has never been found, which is perhaps why his story has never quite been laid to rest. He has been the subject of endless speculation over the years, yet somehow, with each new article or book, the man himself has seemed to recede into the shadows. One fact, though, always makes me smile. The day before he died, in breach of every conceivable regulation, he drove across the border into the Republic and went fishing.

NINETEEN

In the summer of 2000 I was fishing on the Piscatorial Society's stretch of the Avon, a Wiltshire chalk stream. My host was Andrew Buckoke, a very fine angler and the author of *Fishing in Africa*. I thought I was uncompromising about fishing until I met Andrew. He's the kind of fisherman who carries on until it's so dark you can't find the car.

Earlier that year, we had snatched a couple of hours on the Itchen in Hampshire. It was vital that we packed up by six, Andrew told me, because he had a date in London that evening. A first date. A first date so important – and this was almost unheard of – that he was prepared to forgo the evening rise. We were packing up our kit, when, on the far side of a wide pool, a trout rose. A small, discreet rise beneath an overhanging grassy bank. Out of habit we both watched the current and both saw the long silver flash as it came up again.

'Big fish,' I murmured, as Andrew detached his reel from its seating.

'Big fish,' Andrew agreed. 'Why don't you go for him?'

I looked around. There were trees behind us, and it was the best part of thirty yards to the far bank.

'Too far for me,' I said. 'But you could reach him.'

Andrew considered, his reel in one hand and his Hardy fly rod in the other. The fish came up again. He glanced down at his clothes. He had arrived at the river smartly dressed so that he didn't have to go home and change before going to the restaurant. He looked over at the far bank, frowning, and I knew what was going through his mind. If he was going to reach that fish without hooking the trees behind us, he was going to have to wade.

'Do you think I could get away with taking my trousers off?' he asked.

'Could be awkward to explain if another member comes along,' I said.

He nodded and reattached his reel. Kicked off his shoes and socks. Eased himself down the bank. Although the water looked as if it was no more than three feet deep, he was soon up to his waist. Slowly, fly rod in hand, he moved out into the river. After five yards he could go no further without risk of drowning. He began false casting up and down the river and, when he had got almost all his line out, flicked it backhand at the far bank. It unrolled in a long loop; the leader turned over and his fly, a Grey Wulff, alighted a few feet above the trout. It was a dazzling piece of skill, presented as if it were the most ordinary thing in the world. The fish rose in the water, examined the fly and sank down again. With his second cast, Andrew dropped the fly about nine inches above the fish and it came up very fast, almost as a reflex action, taking the Grey Wulff with an audible snap. Five minutes later Andrew was dragging himself, dripping and triumphant, up the bank with the trout thrashing in the net.

'So, how do I look?' he asked as the car door finally closed on our rods and bags and the deceased trout.

'Well,' I said carefully. 'Down to the waist it's all fine. And the shoes are fine too. Would you say she had a good sense of humour?'

Two months later, when we fished the Avon, he was still unattached. It was one of those torpid, breezeless July days. The fish were finicky and difficult, and in obedience to the Piscatorial Society rules, which state that you may cast only to a rising fish, we had spent most of the day watching and waiting. By six o'clock we found ourselves at the bottom end of the half-mile beat, where the water was deep, the banks overgrown and the surface all but motionless. From a pub a couple of fields away, faint snatches of laughter reached us on the evening air.

I was casting to a fish that, a couple of minutes earlier, had made a splashy assault on a moth that was fluttering limply in the surface film. I was using a Coachman, a white-winged fly that had the advantage of being easy to see in the evening light. It didn't seem to interest the trout, though, and when Andrew waved to me I moved on down to where he was.

He'd found a good fish, he told me. Ten yards upstream of where we were standing a mature willow overhung the river, its outer branches dipping in the water. The trout, he pointed with his rod, was lying amongst these. We waited and a minute later there was a tiny dimple of a rise.

'So go for it,' I told him.

'I tried,' he said. 'You have a go.'

I crept backwards and forwards, peering into the darkening river, trying to get a sightline on the place where the fish had risen. But from every angle, it seemed, part of the tree was in the way. That the position was near-impregnable made me even more certain that the fish was a good one. It rose again. A foot upstream of the spreading ripples, willow leaves dragged on the silent current. More trailed a foot below, and the fish lay in the oval looking-glass of water between. I couldn't reach it from the side as there was yet another branch in the way. However, if I moved far enough downstream, I calculated, I might just be able to get an angle on it. Andrew sat on the bank with the net, watching.

It was possible. There was a place from where, if I knelt, I could see the fish's lie through the branches. Whilst it would take the mother of all lucky casts to shoot a fly through that tunnel of leaves, it was still possible. I knotted on a new leader and took out my fly box. There were probably fifty dry flies in there. Some of them were newish patterns that I'd picked up here and there – Adams, Humpy, Cul de Canard – while others were the more traditional Tups, Duns and Olives that I'd used since I was a boy. A fly box, after a decade or two, becomes a kind of aide-mémoire. In mine, amongst others, there's a silvery swarm of Blue Uprights, which takes me straight to the beer-brown stretch of the Exe once owned by the Carnarvon Arms; a battered little mayfly called a Pont Audemer that recalls a magical evening on the Risle in Normandy; a pair of John Storeys, their wings still sprightly, which I haven't used since leaving Ampleforth.

Of the flies in the Loch Leven box that Robert had thrown to me that morning thirty years earlier, most were long gone. Some had caught fish until they unravelled, some had broken off in trees or on riverbeds, and one – a little Blue-Winged Olive – had been extracted from my left ear with a pair of snipe-nose pliers in the outpatients department of Gloucester Hospital. However, there was one fly so exquisite that I'd never used it. It had a creamy hackle and wings, a claret silk body and the long triple tail of the *ephemeridae*. It was, I think, one of the J. W. Dunne patterns that Hardy's sold in their Pall Mall shop until the mid-1960s. This was the fly I reached for now and tied to my leader. I put a drop of waterproofing oil on it and in the fading light watched its transformation to ruby-bodied translucence.

The fish was rising steadily, about once every two or three minutes. I watched as he came up, rocking the ceiling of his olive chamber, and I remembered a pocket handkerchief on a long-ago summer lawn. When I started to cast, it was as if I was doing so in slow motion, threading the line through the elongated enfilade of leaves. The fly struck the bough upstream of the fish and fell to the looking-glass surface. A moment later it vanished in a discreet circlet of ripples.

I struck, and the fish jagged furiously away, a broad black tail slapping the surface so that the shadows crazed. As I attempted to turn it, I knew that this was the biggest river trout I had ever hooked. For several minutes it stayed deep, urgently circling its domain, and then streaked upstream. I brought it back three times, and each time it broke away and raced upstream. Side-strain eventually told, however, and when it surfaced, pectorals fanning angrily beneath the broad olive back, Andrew slipped the net below it and hauled it double-handed out of the river. Seen from side-on, through the dripping mesh, it was suddenly huge. Two feet of shining, black-spotted trout.

'It's a wild fish,' said Andrew. 'That was never born in a hatchery.'

'How big?' I asked, as he unhooked it.

'At least five and a half pounds. Maybe six.'

I don't think we discussed keeping it, or even weighing it. Instead, Andrew lowered the net to the water and quietly drew it away from the fish. The trout worked its gills and fins for a moment in the shallows, then glided majestically away.

Fishing has its disappointments, its frustrations and its blank days, none of which lessen with the passing of the years. There are times when you feel yourself an alien figure in the landscape. Days when, for all your effort and calculation, you just can't read the water. And then there are the times when it all comes right. When the theory falls away, and you and the place are one. Those moments represent a sum of practical experience, although they are also the gift of those who taught you. I understand now why Robert was absolutist in his method, and why he spoke of honour and the dry fly in the same sentence. Because the rules we impose on ourselves are everything – especially in the face of nature, which, for all its outward poetry, is a slaughterhouse. It's not a question of wilfully making things harder, but of a purity of approach without which success has no meaning. And this, ultimately, was his lesson: that the fiercest joy is to be a spectator of your own conduct and find no cause for complaint.

TWENTY

CHALK-STREAM FISHING IS ARCADIAN. A PRIVATE MASQUE, enacted in a dream-world. Everything about it is unreal; everything about it goes against the grain of the age. It's intensely seductive, like all lost-England fantasies, holding something narcotic in its allure. To immerse yourself too often and too deeply is to lose yourself. Real life lies elsewhere.

Thamesmead is in East London, a concrete expanse between the mudflats of Gallions Reach and Erith marshes. It was here that Stanley Kubrick shot *Full Metal Jacket*, and it was on Thamesmead Lake that a thirty-eight-year-old rock musician named René Berg went pike-fishing one steel-skied March morning in 1994. He caught a forty-one-pounder, the biggest London pike ever landed (the previous record was forty pounds, caught in Totteridge Pond in 1797).

I determined to meet René when I heard about this capture and tracked him down to a flat over a garage near the Balls Pond

Road. A dreamy, melancholic figure who had played with a number of bands, including The Idle Flowers and Hanoi Rocks, he was working on a follow-up to his 1992 solo album, which was released under the title of *The Leather, the Loneliness, and Your Dark Eyes*. On the walls of his flat were detailed drawings and paintings of pike. He was a fine, obsessive draughtsman.

He told me about the forty-one-pounder and showed me a photograph of himself cradling the huge, bronze-flanked fish. He'd hardly been able to land it, he told me, as it was too big for the net, and an hour after returning it to the water his hands were still shaking. Afterwards, however, it had been a different story. People he thought were his friends accused him of all sorts of bizarre fabrications – faking the photos, falsifying the weight – and it all began to get him down. For a long time, fishing seemed pointless; the capture of the pike had brought him as much grief as satisfaction and it was inconceivable that he would ever catch a comparable specimen.

With time, however, his enthusiasm had returned. He understood and shared my fascination with decayed urban waterways, with wind-blurred reservoirs, obscure irrigation channels and desolate, graffiti-streaked stretches of canal. I picked him up at dawn a few days later and we drove out to Wanstead Ponds. These vast sheets of water are all that remain of an East London estate that once held one of England's grandest mansions. A painting by William Hogarth, *Assembly at Wanstead House*, shows the building's fabulously ornate interior before it was demolished in 1822 to meet debts. Today, the park is a suburban Illyria, with bluebells in the spring, Shakespeare plays in the summer and a bittersweet air of vanished grandeur. The ornamental lakes have always held big pike, which are pursued with dedication by a handful of secretive, all-weather anglers.

That December morning it was freezing and the water so cold that it burnt the fingers; René, however, was wearing skin-tight latex hipsters and a hand-painted shirt. His eyes, as they scanned the iron-grey acres of lake, bore the suggestion of mascara; having played several sets at a club the night before, he applied himself to the business in hand with fragile intensity. We prepared our baits – frozen sprats – which René injected with a green oil from a bottle in his bag. An hour later, with the vapour still rising from the lake, his float zipped away, the line cutting urgently through the surface film. When he struck, there was a shuddering bow-wave, but the fish was gone, leaving nothing more than a lacerated bait.

Although it was the nearest to a catch that we got that day, the outing seemed to reignite something in René. In the months that followed we went all over London after pike, watching the winter sun rise over Walthamstow Reservoir, Hampstead Ponds, Alexandra Palace Lake, the Grand Union Canal, the River Lea, the Serpentine and, through dark curtains of rain, Thamesmead. Other fishermen joined the hunt, all veterans of winter piking, and sometimes there were as many as half a dozen of us huddled over our thermos flasks. All of us knew the London pike legends, like the one associated with the great Victorian angler Alfred Jardine. When he died in 1910 at the age of eighty-two, *The Field* published a eulogy that included the following tale:

> Previous to its being drawn empty for the canal through a great drought, Ruislip Reservoir contained some monster pike, one of which, weighing 35lb, was captured by a resident at Harrow. But he and other anglers were aware of the presence in the lake of something much larger, among the 'others' being Mr Alfred Jardine, who seemed to possess a strong faculty for getting information of this kind. He told me how he went for this pike and, wonderful to tell, got him on. 'You know,' said J, 'I never fish with less than 150 yards of line when going for big pike, but I might as well have had a reel of cotton, for the beast made a mighty rush and ran my line clean out; I never got the least chance of a turn on him.' When the drought came and the lake was drained…a mass of putrefying fish was left, and amongst the mass was one monster whose weight was estimated at about 50lb.

Whether there's a fifty-pounder swimming in metropolitan waters today is a matter for conjecture. London pike are famously dour and only sheer cussedness kept us at it. I kept an alarm clock set for an hour before dawn, filled the family freezer with unwelcome dead-baits – smelt, sprats, eel tails, herring – and on fishing days accepted spousal banishment to a downstairs sleeping-bag. Early mornings saw me gulping down a cup of scalding tea, dragging the gear out to the car and racing through the near-empty streets to René's eyrie over the garage. From there he would emerge, wild-eyed beneath his bags and rods, and we would hurry on to our chosen destination. Even if it was pouring with rain these were heady occasions, successive sets of traffic lights flickering to green as we swept past in a daze of sleep-deprived optimism. This, surely, had to be the day.

We had our successes. I caught an eight-pounder, early one morning, in the canal below the Daewoo garage in Camden Town, and René took a slightly larger fish in the Serpentine in Hyde Park. He was kneeling to return it when an imposing figure in Saudi Arabian robes passed by.

'Is that your pet?' he asked, indicating the pike.

'Yes,' said René. The man nodded and moved on.

A week later he approached René at the same spot. 'Where's your pet?' he demanded, his tone severe.

'Swimming,' René reassured him.

But we didn't catch our big London pike. Day after day, the optimism of dawn gave way to the monochrome reality of noon. Of rainswept, litter-strewn walkways, chain-smoking kids with straining bull terriers, and gnomic oldsters telling us we should have been there last week because some bloke had a twenty-pounder out – claims that we knew to be lies because we'd been there last week.

One morning at Thamesmead there were five of us out. A satellite TV crew turned up, hoping for some big-fish action, and set up their gear. After many damp and eventless hours had passed, finally line began to whisper off my reel. Rousing the TV people, by then catatonic with boredom, I wound in a tiny, affronted pike of just over two pounds. I think we all knew at that moment that the game was up: that it wasn't going to happen for us. Nothing was said, but we never fished as a group again.

Winter became spring, the pike season ended and I lost touch with René. That autumn, as the temperature fell and the days began to draw in, I tried his old numbers but there was no response. It was only some months later that I learnt that he had died; alcohol, heroin and depression, it seemed, had all played their part. I knew very little about him, when all was said and done, but I recognized a fellow spirit behind the glam-rock trappings. There's something about a man fired by a boyhood passion, a fervour that adult experience never fully occludes. That winter, fishing on the Test, I caught a pike of twenty-one pounds – a huge fish – and tried without success to imagine one of twice its size. That London could support the monster that René caught tells us something about the city: that there are still corners illuminated by darkness. There is still a Venice of the Black Sea.

London pike fishermen, like their quarry, tend to be lone wolves and you don't see many on the canal these days. The fish are there, though, as they've always been. As I discover that freezing night behind King's Cross, when, sometime long before dawn, the line begins, inch by inch, to tick from my reel. Deep down, something is moving, and I know that this is the moment, this is why we do it. For that heart-slamming infinity. For the knowledge that, this time, it might not be a fish at all.

ACKNOWLEDGEMENTS

My thanks to the historian Turtle Bunbury, a generous fund of information on 15/19th The King's Royal Hussars, the regiment in which his grandfather Lord Rathdonnell and my father served in the Second World War. Guy Courage's history of the regiment from 1939 to 1945 was also a valuable source. Concerning the career of Robert Nairac, I am indebted to John Parker's *Death of a Hero* and Martin Dillon's *The Dirty War*, two of the very few accounts untainted by propaganda or fantasy. To those who spoke to me about Robert but have preferred to remain nameless, my thanks also.

Echoes of the 'great debate' at the Fly Fishers Club in 1938 are audible to this day; for those wishing to know more, Terry Lawton's *Nymph Fishing* and Andrew Herd's *The Fly* will be early ports of call. Many art historians have written about Claud Lorrain's *Landscape with the Nymph Egeria*, but few as perceptively as Michael Kitson; a transcript of his magisterial 1966

Charlton Lecture about the painting is held at the University of Newcastle-upon-Tyne. For information on the history and theory of Chaos Magic, Phil Hine is the author to seek out. For friends and fans of René Berg, a well-tended tribute site exists at www.myspace.com/reneberg.

LJ, 2009